THE SACRED ART OF SELF-DECEPTION

SPIRITUALITY

THE SACRED SERIES
BOOK 1

SHADOW EASTON

LUCAS EASTON

Copyright © 2025 by Katana Publishing LLC, Sacramento, CA

All rights reserved.

No part of this book may be reproduced in any form or by any electronic or mechanical means, including information storage and retrieval systems, without written permission from the author, except for the use of brief quotations in a book review.

NO AI TRAINING: Without in any way limiting the author's [and publisher's] exclusive rights under copyright, any use of this Publication and its contents to "train" generative artificial intelligence (AI) technologies to generate text or Frameworks is expressly prohibited. The author reserves all rights to license uses of this work for generative AI training and the development of machine learning language models.

Print ISBN: 979-8-9906182-7-5

E-Book ISBN: 979-8-9906182-8-2

DISCLAIMER

Our society has a belief in sickness. As such, we have the medical industrial complex as well as battalions of attorneys that work to ensure that the medical establishment is believed to be the only authority on the subject of health and sickness. To comply with their requirements, we must include the following.

The Authors provide the Book, information, content and/or data (collectively, "Information") contained therein for informational purposes only. The Authors do not provide any medical advice in the Book and the Information should not be so construed or used. Nothing contained in the Book is intended to create a physician-patient relationship, to replace the services of a licensed, trained physician or health professional or to be a substitute for medical advice of a physician or trained health professional licensed in your state. Do not rely on anything contained in the Book, and consult a physician licensed in your state in all matters relating to your health. You hereby agree that you shall not make any health or medical-related decision based in whole or in part on anything contained in the Book.

The Authors are not responsible for the reader's emotional or physical reactions to anything in this book, including but not limited to:

Anxiety, Anger, Heart Palpitations, Emotional Pain or Suffering, Spiritual Psychosis, Identity Crisis, Depression, Loss of Appetite, Digestive Issues, Blood Pressure Readings, Paranoia, Sudden Onset Critical Thinking, Psychosis of any kind, Mood Disorders, Feelings of Bliss, Truth-Realization, Mystical Experiences of any kind, Ear Ringing, Body Aches, Symptoms of any kind, Alien Abduction, Anal Probes, U.T.I's, Hormone levels, Allergic reactions of any kind, Physical and/or emotional issues of any kind.

Neither the authors nor the publisher assumes any responsibility for errors, omissions, or contrary interpretations of the subject matter herein. Any perceived slight of any individual or organization is purely unintentional and is not to be considered hate speech of any kind. Brand and product names are trademarks or registered trademarks of their respective owners.

BUSHIDO - BULLSHIDO - BULLSHITTO

Decoding BULLSHITTO: How did we get here?

In a eureka moment, amidst the labyrinth of complex texts and the quest for a theme for the first book in 'The Sacred Series,' inspiration struck us. Our martial arts journey, steeped in the tradition of Bushido — the esteemed samurai code of feudal Japan, emphasizing loyalty, honor, and martial arts — provided the perfect muse.

Drawing from Inazo Nitobe's insights, we revered the samurai's seven guiding rules:

Righteousness, Loyalty, Honor, Respect, Honesty, Courage, and Consistency.

These were the guiding principles not only of the art but of life.

Through the years, the martial arts world witnessed a dilution of its sacred ethos, morphing noble arts into a carnival of "Bullshido" — a term coined to label the circus of faux mastery and charlatanism.

Bullshido

The term Bullshido gained popularity to describe the desecration of the original Bushido.

> "Martial arts instructions that are fraudulent, inept, or otherwise not worth trusting.
> If the instructor appears to be out to make money, then the chances are that you will probably encounter Bullshido."

– Urban Dictionary by Light Joker, March 27, 2007 –

Observing the spiritual marketplace's chaos, it's clear the apple hasn't fallen far from the dojo.

Welcome to the Wild West of the Spiritual Bazaar, where spiritual narcissism rides high, and authenticity is as rare as a unicorn at a donkey show.

Behold the landscape littered with imposters, faux gurus, pseudo-teachers, counterfeit wisdom, bogus enlightenment, and a parade of phony claims, teaching, knowledge, secrets, courses, and enlightenment.

An all-you-can-eat buffet of spiritual fast food designed to fatten the Ego while starving TRUTH.

From the moment you embark on this journey, you're sold the dream of awakening, enlightenment, and a one-way ticket to Nirvanaville—always just one more expensive seminar away.

If you've ever felt like you're navigating a maze of spiritual McDojos, where every corner hides a new brand of enlightened charlatan peddling salvation for the low, low price of your sanity, you have come to the right place.

Enter BULLSHITTO, the dojo for the discerning Truth Samurai who's had enough of the fluff. Armed with the katana of skepticism and shielded by a no-nonsense approach to spiritual growth, you're about to cut through the crap with the precision of a laser-guided truth missile.

It takes guts, grit, and a hefty dose of reality to navigate this path — a path where courage, respect, honesty, and consistency are not just virtues but your very survival tools.

Prepare to dive headfirst into the spiritual dumpster fire with eyes wide open, separating the sacred from the scam with the skill of a seasoned con artist's worst nightmare.

Because, in the quest for TRUTH, BULLSHITTO is not just a challenge; it's an initiation into the sacred art of calling out nonsense by its name.

Let the Games begin.

CONTENTS

Foreword	15
DINNER WITH JIM	21
THE SPIRITUAL SHOPPING MALL	25
OLD AGE RELIGIONS	29
BLIND BELIEF	51
ARCHANGELS	57
NEW AGE SPIRITUALITY	63
SPIRITUAL MALL SELF- CHECKOUT	111
MIND DOJO	115
PERCEIVED REALITY	117
LIMITATIONS IN THE GAME	125
MIND DOJO	145
POSSIBILITIES IN THE GAME	147
MIND DOJO	163
NATURAL DEVELOPMENT INTO ADULTHOOD VS. ENLIGHTENMENT	165
EGO STRUCTURE	169
THOUGHTS AND THINKING	179
MIND DOJO	193
BELIEFS	197
MIND DOJO	213
EMOTIONS AND FEELINGS	217
MIND DOJO	229
THE DOME CONCEPT	231
THE EGO-CHARACTER DOME IN 'REAL LIFE'	237
MIND DOJO	249
GAME RECAP	253
SACRED SELF-DECEPTION	261
ACKNOWLEDGMENTS	265

FOREWORD

This is the first book in the Sacred Series. It is a primer. These ideas and concepts are foundational to begin to understand the Ego-character and where it fits in the larger scheme of things.

This book deals with natural development into adulthood. To do that, all the beliefs we hold must be questioned. We've taken aim directly at spiritual and religious beliefs because they are the easiest to dissect from a developmental perspective.

This book is full of humor, sarcasm, and deep meaning. From our experience now, it's easy to see the humor in all the beliefs and ideologies and in society at large. It has all become quite comical, and we can't take it seriously any longer.

We do understand that some of our readers won't see the humor because they take these things very seriously; we remember how that was too. Our intent is not to offend out of a mean spirit; it is only to bring a humorous light to shine on subjects that no one else will.

Perhaps no one else can. We have the utmost love and respect for people, but we no longer have the ability to respect the beliefs they hold onto. If there are strong emotional reactions to anything in this book, it simply proves the points we are making.

We want our readers to know that it's absolutely okay to look at things differently. It's okay to ask the hard questions, and it's okay to laugh about our own ignorance, gullibility, and naïveté, especially when we haven't been given the right tools to figure anything out.

Whenever we are being taught to use a new tool, we aren't really good at it in the beginning. It's like learning how to use chopsticks if you weren't raised in a household where that was an everyday tool. You do the best you can with the information you've got, but then a bona fide chopstick professional sits next to you and shows you how they do it. They can pick up anything with those things while we struggle to get a single grain of rice into our mouths.

When the professional shows you, he not only demonstrates how but also explains why he does it that way. Suddenly, you have a new tool that you can become proficient at using.

The tool we'll be trying to teach you to use differently is your mind. We want you to hone your samurai sword of discernment and cut through the nonsense like the warrior you are. This book is not about telling anyone what to think; it's simply pointing out how to think critically for yourself.

When we use the term **'the Truth of One'** throughout this book, we are writing from the undeniable realization that there is only one thing, and we are calling that thing Truth or Consciousness. Truth cannot be divided, nor can it be reduced any further. Truth cannot change, nor can it be claimed or it isn't truth. This is the foundation we are using to impart ideas around who we think we are, how the "I" came to be and the structure it runs on.

FOREWORD

We don't offer any paths to the compassionate heart, no tips on raising your frequency or vibration. We don't advocate for only positive thoughts, and you won't find your way to heaven, ascension, or nirvana.

You won't suddenly burst into infinite bliss; you won't get pampered. We are not teachers, gurus, or priests. You won't find channeled messages, and you won't meet your spirit guides. We don't sell unity consciousness, and we have no contact with anyone in the Galactic Federation. We may, however, be able to provide a discount code for Sunseeds.

We write about beliefs and why they should be handled with care. We write about the silliness of society and some of the more explosive topics that not many people will touch, like culture.

We write from our own authority, our own experience, and our own understanding of what the supposed 'ancient' texts have been trying to describe for thousands of years. We do not claim to know everything, nor do we claim that anything in this book is infallible.

We write with the understanding that no matter how much we think we know, life is a rich, intimate, sacred mystery that can't be dissected or conceptualized and doesn't fit into any box that our minds build for it. We fully embrace the unknowing. We don't have cool accessories or courses to sell, and rituals are not required.

We have tried to write the book that we wish we would have had when we started the journey. We would have appreciated some in-your-face talk about the bullshit we believed in.

FOREWORD

This book is for anyone who has heard that little voice telling them that something is missing and that it can be found. It's for the people who keep running on the spiritual hamster wheel and never catch the carrot they're chasing. It's for people who want to wake up and smell the bullshit so they can remove it. It's for people who are tired of living the same day over and over again and wonder why their life never changes.

It's for people who want raw, radical honesty. It's for people who are searching in all the wrong places for the one thing that can't be lost.

This first book in this series is our attempt to point out some of the things we had to question, consider, and let go of to get off the spiritual merry go round.

Come have a little fun with us, bring your sense of humor and your samurai sword, and let's have a rollicking good time looking at our self-deceptions.

Shadow & Lucas Easton

"It's the truth I'm after, and the truth never harmed anyone.
What harms us is to persist in self-deceit and ignorance."

- Marcus Aurelius -

DINNER WITH JIM

We met our friend Jim, whom we hadn't seen in a few years, for dinner. The change in his appearance was striking. The last time we saw him, he was buttoned up, clean-shaven, wearing suits and ties, and was the CEO of a fairly large company. This evening, he showed up in organic cotton baggy pants, long, slightly greasy-looking hair tied up in a man bun, a scraggly beard that hadn't seen a trim in a very long time, a colorful woven hoodie-type shirt, and sandals. It was quite a transformation.

We sat down to have dinner together and began chatting about the superficial things as folks do, then the waiter came to take our order. Jim had a hard time finding something to eat on the menu because he informed us that he had taken a vow not to eat any meat because animals are conscious beings.

With that as his guide, and after a long conversation with the waiter about cooking methods, his order was finally placed for something he felt okay about eating because it wasn't a sentient being.

This act of ordering a meal opened up the conversation so that Jim could share with us the 'transformation' that he had gone through over the last few years. "I went to a spiritual retreat, and that changed my life. You know I've always been interested in the spiritual side of life, and I needed to find a practice to jump-start my journey. I no longer eat meat so that my vessel can be purified. I try to eat a lot of 'living food,' you know, fruits, vegetables, and nuts so that I can absorb the life energy into my body."

"I had a Feng Shui consultant set up a meditation room in my house; it's amazing, a real sanctuary. I have an altar, the right color candles set up in the proper directional sequence for optimum energy flow, a water fountain, and several crystals to help protect the energy of the space. I've got singing bowls, special incense imported from India, and a great collection of mandala art on the walls. I really love having my sacred space."

"Wow, Jim, how much time do you spend in your meditation room?" I ask. "I'm up to about 4 hours a day now!"

"That retreat really gave me the foundation for my spiritual rituals, and I think they're really helping." "Helping with what?" I ask. "You know, my spiritual journey. I'm unblocking my chakras, purifying myself, and clearing my karmic debt. I've been volunteering at several meaningful charities doing really great work where I get to practice my loving-kindness and compassion."

We are dumbfounded by this; we look at each other and Lucas asks, "Jim, let me ask you a question." Jim enthusiastically says, "Sure! I'd love to share!" Lucas takes a beat and then simply says, "Why?" Jim responds, "What do you mean?" looking confused. Lucas replies, "Why are you doing all of these things?" Jim looks even more confused. "I'm doing this for my spiritual journey, so I can 'level up' on the path," he says. "What path? Where is this path supposed to lead you?" Lucas asks. "You know, the PATH. Purifying my body and mind so I can hold higher vibrational consciousness." Ever persistent, Lucas says, "And where does holding higher vibrational consciousness get you? How many hours of meditation a day will be sufficient for this higher vibrational consciousness? What IS the purpose of higher vibrational consciousness? Is this a Buddha thing or what?" Jim is getting uncomfortable. "There's only one Buddha," he replies, "but this level of practice is important to get to the next step on my spiritual path toward Unity Consciousness."

Jim is stuck where most people are, doing ridiculous things for some pie-in-the-sky idea that always remains just out of reach. In his response of "there's only one Buddha," he is really making the point that whatever Buddhist tradition or 'practice' he is following isn't producing more Buddhas. Perhaps that's why they call it 'practicing' Buddhism in the first place, because no one is good at it, and no one is finding Nirvana.

The entire unity consciousness thing is as incorrect as the rest of it, but Jim has dedicated his life now to chasing this carrot. Jim is sitting in his pimped-out meditation room for several hours a day, waiting for something to happen to him that can only happen through him.

This type of spiritual nonsense isn't just found in the various Buddhist-type practices; it's everywhere. It's in all the 'major' religions: Eastern, Western, or New Age; it doesn't matter; they are all based on belief and not fact. Yep, we just said that all religion, new or old, is all bullshit. It is a lie perpetuated generation after generation, and at the end of the day, they are all the same.

They are all based on separation. They all have some form of the reward/punishment system and some kind of 'savior' archetype. They all point to somewhere else to go and they all promise some kind of heaven, nirvana, ascension, or 5D, with mansions, crowns, or a bunch of virgins and promises of redemption and atonement.

They all require you to subjugate your power to an outside authority: God, priest, teacher, guru, or prophet. You can't possibly understand the intricacies of these teachings, so you must have certified authorities to interpret them for you. It makes us question who the FIRST authority was if we need one now to understand it, but we'll never know that answer.

We're going to take a fun, hard look at these things in this book. Some of you may feel offended at some point, and if so, that means we've done our job. Our intent here is to look closely at our belief systems, to question, to dissect, to see our own assumptions, to bring light to the murky waters, and to have a lot of fun doing it.

It's important to understand that we are looking at the structure of beliefs, not personally attacking the believer. This isn't personal. If you find yourself getting triggered by anything in this book, we encourage you to keep reading. We have the utmost love and respect for the believers; we do not, however, hold any respect for the belief itself, except as a brilliant construct of Ego that makes this amazing experience of life possible.

It is our hope that you will take this journey with a light heart and a sense of humor and come out the other side with some clarity that can actually change your life.

THE SPIRITUAL SHOPPING MALL

In our view, the entire religious and spiritual situation we have today is nothing more than a large shopping mall. It has every kind of store selling whatever kind of carrot you find appealing to chase.

The herd enters the mall and then branches off into the stores that have just the right sparkle and dazzle and advertise freedom from suffering, a better life, or hope after death. The herd is still the herd and safely kept within the confines of the mall, but they all feel special, like they are 'going their own way' and that they're really getting somewhere. It is a brilliant design to keep you right where you are while making you feel like you are progressing on some path to somewhere else.

It is fascinating to us to look at all the myriads of teachings within the spiritual mall. You've got such a selection! Traditional religion, Buddhism, and the law of attraction manifestation crowd have the largest stores; they're the big-box anchor stores in the mall.

Then you have the 'we're all transitioning to 5D at the same time' folks, the personal growth seminar celebrities, churches built around New Age nonsense, the 'let's get in touch with our dead relatives' folks, the folks who channel 'higher dimensional beings,' and more ascended masters than you can shake a stick at.

In many cases, the sales pitch includes an 'Ancient Secret' or some other type of mystical, unknown-until-today 'knowledge.' The list is endless, and it's an awesome demonstration of just how the game is rigged so that your chances of Awakening are slim to none.

New Age Spirituality is as much bullshit as the major religions; it's just wrapped differently. It's Religion 2.0, and they use the same methods to build their following. It's a well-laid-out business model, and it works.

The seeking is endless. Why do we spend so much time, energy and money on endless seeking? The answer to this question is simple; Ego Character is the seeker. It seeks validation, meaning, salvation and the granddaddy of them all, the 'enlightenment' badge. It is itself an illusory process that operates in a structure, but we generally identify AS this process, never seeing the fiction that it is. That's not right, wrong, good, or bad. It's just the structure of this experience.

The Spiritual Ego is often the hardest to see because the seeking seems noble, the messages provide a meaningful narrative and most offer some sort of continuity of existence after death. Who doesn't want that? When we really look at the offerings in our Spiritual Industrial Complex, we'll see the workings of Ego in all its glory.

Points to remember as you read: Ego requires the illusion of separation; meaning a "me" in here and everything else out there. Ego requires a story; "I'm getting somewhere that is better than what is here and now." Ego requires continuity; "I will remain in some form after death." Ego requires ownership; "I am doing the necessary work to gain enlightenment or salvation."

With that in mind, let's start with a brief look at some of the major religions in the mall; they're the most common with the largest customer base. They have anchored the mall for centuries and have high customer retention rates. We're just going to touch on the marketing basics in a very simplistic way.

OLD AGE RELIGIONS

CHRISTIANITY

Protestant Christians believe that Jesus died for our sins and that believing in Jesus is the only way to "salvation" and the only way you can go to heaven when you die. Using the Bible as their authority, the premise is that everyone is born in "sin." God requires a sacrifice for sin, and so he sent his Son Jesus, (who is also God) to die a horrible death for you so that you can go to heaven. You are born a sinner, and you will go to hell unless you believe in Jesus and "ask him into your heart," and then you are saved from eternal damnation. According to this doctrine, we all deserve death.

There is a hefty price to pay for the great sin of being born, yet the folks who believe this generally have the most children.

How cruel is that? These folks will tell you they believe that all human life is sacred. Human life is sacred, but humans are all born sinners and are on their way to eternal damnation unless they repent and believe in Jesus. So, these folks are popping out kids while truly believing that there's a chance these kids will be punished in hell for all eternity. What a dichotomy.

The magic prayer of asking Jesus into your heart, though, will do the trick. What, exactly, does 'asking Jesus into your heart' mean? It's not directly in the Bible, but somehow it refers to the belief that Jesus is the Son of God.

So, if you say a little prayer to Jesus and tell him you believe that he's the Son of God and that you know that you are a sinner because you were born and ask him to save you from an eternity in hell, he will.

You will then be assured of going to heaven with streets of gold, mansions and crowns and stuff. All you have to do is believe.

Here's a little personal magical prayer that will evidently save you from eternal damnation, taken from the back of a Gideon Bible:

"God, from my heart, I admit to You that I m a sinner and I ask for Your forgiveness. I believe that Your son Jesus, took the punishment I deserve by shedding His blood on the cross. He gave His life as the full payment for my sins and rose again from the dead. Thank you for changing my heart. I now confess and turn from my sins and receive Your Son, Jesus as my Savior and Lord. – Amen."

Take special note of the phrase '...**punishment I deserve**...'. This is the basis of the entire religion. On one hand, God loves you, but on the other, you deserve to be punished severely for existing. The saving part seems to be the least stringent of all the major big-box religions, though.

It's really the best version of the fairytale, in our opinion because it doesn't really require anything else—just belief. You are strongly encouraged to give your money to the church and be a good person and try really hard not to sin anymore, because you've already committed the greatest sin, which is being born in the first place.

You don't have to do these things; it's just strongly encouraged. Once you're saved, you can't lose it in most Protestant Christian beliefs. That's a pretty good deal! You buy it once, and it lasts forever. The price of a torturous, violent death for you being born has already been paid! YAY!

Many of the Protestant Christian religions also believe in the rapture. This is the idea that at some point in 'end times', that Christ will come in the clouds and the believers will be sucked up into the sky, both the living and the dead. If you're raised in this as a child, you're constantly afraid of your mom being sucked out of the car and seeing your dead grandma shooting up out of the ground. Talk about abandonment issues!

The reason for this 'rapture' is so that believers don't have to go through the 'tribulation' when the Anti- Christ comes and gives everyone the mark of the beast and such. But the denominations all disagree on the timing of this magical event. Some believe it's before the tribulation, and others believe it's in the middle, and still others believe that it's after. We're not sure what the point would be for it to happen after the hell on earth that the tribulation describes, but those who believe this probably don't know either.

There are various denominations within the Protestant Christian religions; it's a real smorgasbord of fun stuff. From speaking in tongues to serpent handling to the more traditional, stoic worshipers, there's something for everyone. Some teach that women shouldn't wear pants or cut their hair and should be basically seen and not heard except when screaming during childbirth. In others, women can hold leadership positions in the church. In still others, all sexual orientations and/or gender identities are welcome to lead the flock.

From a marketing perspective, Protestant Christianity is the easiest sell of the big-box religions. You can either target the audience at large or niche down and really find your 'sweet spot'. The rules for salvation are pretty simple and not overly stringent, and they have the reward of heaven as the spoonful of sugar to make the bullshit go down.

The Protestant church's main focus is on the resurrection part of the Jesus story. They still use the cross as their logo, but they like to emphasize resurrection. The empty tomb is hard to put in a recognizable, high-converting logo, so the cross was the better choice. Their cross logo is usually without the bloody, beaten Jesus on it though, so it's a little less morbid than the Catholic version. Eternal life without all the messy, bloody, creepy death stuff. Heaven sells.

CATHOLICISM

Catholics are considered Christians, but Catholics have more magic and swag than the Protestants. While Christians believe that they are saved by faith alone, Catholics are a little more rigorous on this point. Catholics say it requires baptism, faith, good works, and remaining in a state of grace (being in good standing with the Catholic Church, and participation in the sacraments).

You don't necessarily just get to go to heaven as a Catholic either; you might need a stop-off in purgatory to purify yourself *through pain* before you get to meet the Big Guy. But if you're not 'saved' at all, you go straight to hell.

Catholics also have saints that you can pray to. We aren't sure why you would pray to dead guys, but you can if you want. They also hail Mary as the mother of God, and you can pray to her too. Maybe she can intercede with her son for you. We aren't sure if Jesus thinks that's cool; how would you like it if everyone called your mom to try to get you to do something?

The priests and hierarchy of the Catholic Church are another stark difference with Protestant Christianity. The priests have the power to forgive you. That's some crazy shit. They can forgive your sins, and all you have to do is tell them about it and then go and say a magic mantra over and over again while you rub some magic beads and sprinkle yourself with magic water.

(We wonder if the magic water is the same as the magic soccer water that they squirt on 'injured' soccer players that makes them immediately jump up as if nothing happened. We're not sure we'll ever know.)

Catholics like the Bible, but they don't use it as their only authority. Their authority also comes from their very own church traditions passed down through all those years. It's amazing that the church found the time to pass down and teach traditions when they were so busy torturing and murdering folks for heresy for hundreds of years. But apparently, they did, and through that created their own authority.

This self-appointed authority led to the Inquisition, a horrific time in history when they used this authority to execute anyone who didn't follow their rules or believe in their version of the fairy tale. During this time, the sixth commandment of **'Thou Shalt Not Kill'** was clearly thrown out as non-applicable.

That's what you get to do with your own authority: take only what furthers your agenda and leave the rest. If they would have had a marketing firm, we think the slogan in those days would be something like "Buy or Die!" It's short, catchy, and to the point, and extremely effective at getting people to buy the bullshit you're selling. It's kind of like the Steve Jobs Apple campaign; they sell emotion and experience not iPhones. It doesn't get much more emotional than fear of death—Steve would have been proud.

The Catholic religion is a hard sell; they don't even really get on the 'heaven is paved with streets of gold' gig. They sell heaven as constant worship of and union with God, the ultimate end and fulfillment of the deepest human longings, the state of supreme, definitive happiness. This doesn't really sound that sexy, but it must work since they are the richest religion by far. People keep buying, so they keep selling.

Catholics also tend to have a lot of children; we are confused as to why they feel the need to continue to bring people into the world to suffer through the tenets of the church to avoid hell, but also with the possibility of purgatory? Seems rather cruel, but it does keep the funds flowing in.

The Catholic Church is also much more focused on the death part of the Jesus story. Their cathedrals are built on the bones of their priests, and they regularly display the cross with the bloody, broken Jesus still on it. It's a death cult wrapped in amazing architecture and stained glass. They continually reinforce the death of Jesus and then tell you it's okay to pray to his mother. How would you feel if your child died in a horrific manner, and someone took a picture of the gruesome death and put it up on every corner for people to gawk at? We're not sure Mother Mary is a big fan of this kind of fear-mongering manipulation.

In spite of the death focus, the Catholic Church is still going strong. It's all in the marketing. The public relations arm of this church is so brilliant that they can still get you to let your child be an altar boy despite all the well-documented rampant sexual depravity and abuse. You can sell anything to the masses with just the right marketing campaign.

MORMONISM

The Mormon religion is another fun thing to explore. It didn't exist until 1830. When Joseph Smith was 17, he had an 'angelic vision' and supposedly received ancient records written in 'reformed Egyptian' from the heavenly messenger Moroni, which he translated by the 'gift and power of God' into the Book of Mormon. These 'sacred' writings chronicle God's dealings with his people in the Western Hemisphere.

Basically, he decided that he had a better take on the teachings of Christianity for an American audience. He was, if nothing else, a brilliant branding and marketing guy. The Western Hemisphere was simply left out of all the traditional 'Bible' religions and so it was definitely an underserved market. It really is a brilliant story and should be studied in business schools. Find a niche that isn't served, write a book, be a charismatic rebel, create a personal brand, and sell it to the hungry souls just looking for their place in all of this religion stuff. All of a sudden, America has a central role in the story!

For example, he taught that the Garden of Eden from the Bible was in Jackson County, Missouri and when God banished Adam and Eve, they had to go all the way to another county! God banished them to Daviess County, Missouri according to Smith, which is about 87 miles away. Must have been a tough journey.

The Book of Mormon is marketed as *another* testament of Jesus Christ. It created its own authority much like the Catholic traditions did. They also have their own path to heaven, or in their case, heavens. Their heaven has three levels: celestial, terrestrial, and telestial.

The celestial kingdom is the realm of Heavenly Father, Jesus Christ, and the Holy Ghost. To get all the way there, you must believe in Jesus, be baptized in the Mormon church, continually repent, sustain and support the Mormon prophets, receive the Mormon ordinances (such as baptism for the dead and eternal marriage in a Mormon temple), and live faithfully according to the commandments.

The terrestrial kingdom is a place for people who are deceived into rejecting the Mormon gospel in their mortal lives but accept it in the spirit world.

The telestial kingdom is the destination for the multitudes of wicked people who reject the Mormon gospel both in mortality and in the spirit world. Evidently, before you even get to this kingdom, you are sent to 'hell' where you suffer for your sins before being released after the end of the Millennium.

(Institute for Religious Research, The Mormon View of Heaven and Hell, The Bottom-Line Guide to Mormonism, Part 15 by: Robert M. Bowman Jr. Post Date: August 26, 2013)

The good news is that just about everyone gets to go to one of the kingdoms! YAY! So that's an easier sell than the run-of-the-mill heaven or hell. The bad news is to get to the lowest kingdom, you have to do a thousand years in hell first. The even worse news is that to get to the highest kingdom requires knowing four secret handshakes, which we are not privy to.

The Mormon Church also has some magical beliefs. The leaders of the church can and do receive new 'revelations' from God; this is great so that the religion doesn't become stagnant.

The whole baptism for the dead and the eternal marriage stuff is also full of magic; how could they not be? The entire religion is based on a magical 'angelic' visit and interpretation of the message —channeling before it was mainstream!

The Mormons also have special underwear with symbols stitched on them, which they call temple garments. According to an article in the New York Times by Ruth Graham published on July 21, 2021, women find them uncomfortable and itchy and long for buttery soft fabric because their "vaginas need to breathe." Further, there was a quote in the article that said, "People are scared to be brutally honest, to say: 'This isn't working for me. It isn't bringing me closer to Christ; it's giving me U.T.I.s."

Considering the size of the Mormon Church, if you could design and manufacture comfy temple garments, you would have a ready-made market. This is a million-dollar idea. You're welcome.

We just think it's fascinating how religions are started and then take on a life of their own.

Joseph Smith was a rebel; he called himself a prophet, wrote a book, gathered some followers, and boom! We have a whole new religion! But this religion now also requires its teachers to be certified as authorities to teach the masses. See how that works? The rebel changes it up, but the sheep simply follow the predetermined pattern for religion and belief systems. If we had more rebels and fewer sheep, it might make all of this more interesting.

Imagine if someone came up with a newer, new version of the Mormon religion today. A guy gets a message from God, writes a book, and when he takes it to the church, they call him a heretic and throw him in a loony bin because he's obviously mentally ill. If he isn't taken to the loony bin, he may be a charismatic guy and attract followers who really believe in his ideas.

They set up a little compound and live out their version of the newer, new version of the religion, but it has elements in it that are apparently against Federal Law. So, we end up with the FBI surrounding the compound, and it all ends in a bloody shootout.

In fairness, the Mormon Church rebranded itself to the "Church of Jesus Christ of Latter-Day Saints" in 2018, and this rebranding was supposedly because the president of the church receives revelations directly from God. God told him to change the name. No loony bin or bloody shootout for him. If it comes from within the leadership, it must be from God and therefore must be true; but if you receive a channeled message and are NOT a leader of the church, you are clearly delusional.

The obvious cannot be overlooked here. The message from 'God' was most likely that the church no longer wanted to be associated with the darker side of its history. Things like polygamy, which in the early days was taught to be more important than baptism for securing salvation. Under this doctrine, women were only able to be 'saved' by sealing themselves to a man. We are using the term 'women' lightly here, as some of these 'women' were prepubescent. Joseph Smith is said to have had anywhere from 30 to 48 wives! He was clearly extremely dedicated to doing the Lord's work of 'saving women.'

When big brands rebrand, it's generally to better suit the modern public. So, whether it's a message from God or not, it appears to be a simple rebranding to separate themselves from past doctrine that doesn't fly in modern society.

ISLAM

Islam is also an interesting religion to look at. Muslims believe that Islam was revealed over 1,400 years ago in Makkah, Arabia, through a man called Muhammad. He is believed by Muslims to be the last prophet sent by God (Allah).

They believe that God sent prophets to mankind to teach them how to live according to His law. Jesus, Moses, and Abraham are also respected prophets. Their main book is the Qur'an, believed to be the work of Allah as dictated to Muhammad through the Angel Gabriel. Again, channeling before it was mainstream!

There are five pillars of Islam:

- The declaration of faith that there is no God but Allah and that Muhammad is his last messenger.
- Praying three to five times a day, at special times facing Makkah.
- Giving money to charity. Muslims who have money must give a percentage to charity or to the less fortunate.
- Fasting during the lunar month of Ramadan.
- A pilgrimage to Makkah at least once in a lifetime. This is apparently only required if you have the money.

They believe in God, his angles, his books, his messengers, the Last Day, and Fate. Their version of God is also the one God who created the universe and everything in it. They believe in all the messengers or prophets that predate Muhammad, but for some reason, Muhammad is the last messenger.

We are not sure why God stopped channeling messages through angels at the time of Muhammad, but maybe he just didn't have anything more to say; who knows? It's a little suspect, though and creates the illusion of unquestionable 'authority' when you say that your message is the last one, and so anyone who comes after you is a heretic. No Joseph Smiths in Islam, we guess.

Islam is similar to the Catholic Church in that they conquered their way to adoption. Military conquest for the one true God is the most effective marketing method we've seen to date. In the early days of their expansion, it wasn't the "Buy or Die" marketing campaign that we saw with the Catholic Inquisition; it was more monetary in nature, and they didn't force people to convert, but if you didn't, you paid a higher tax. Kind of like the 'sin tax' we have today.

In modern times, the religion seems to have taken a hard line from Alice in Wonderland: "Off with their heads!" as its marketing strategy.

Islam also has the whole heaven and hell structure. They teach that after we die, we will be raised up again for judgment by Allah. Then we will either be rewarded with eternity in heaven or punished with eternity in hell.

The soul's journey is something like this: a person dies, their soul is taken by the angel of death, two angels question the soul, and then the soul enters a state of waiting until the Day of Judgment by Allah.

Heaven is described as an infinite garden that is lush and green, and beneath the gardens, there are streams of milk, honey, and wine. One may drink from them without filling up or being intoxicated. Whatever type of meat is desired will be freshly provided; it is unclear if pork is on the menu in heaven.

A man will be rewarded with seventy or so beautiful young women who are subjected to him. Their heaven is a very sensual experience, and there are references to fine clothes, jewels, and thrones as well.

Similar to the Mormons, the Muslim heaven has levels. Some say there are seven levels of heaven, while others don't number the levels but simply say "many" levels. What we find interesting in the above description of heaven is that while Muslims are forbidden to drink wine on earth, they get a whole river of it in paradise!

So, a great selling point is that if you obey Allah's laws on earth, your reward will be a huge party with an all-you-can-drink open bar!

You still can't get shit-faced, though, as you drink it without being intoxicated, so what's the point?

The idea of getting 70 or so beautiful young women is an interesting one and most likely a major selling point. That would be a high-converting ad campaign in heterosexual men's magazines. In researching this idea, the question, of course, came up: what do women get? There were some interesting takes on this from various question and answer websites. One that caught our attention was a question-and-answer found on *aboutislam.net*.

Question: *"I was just thinking, I am not 100% sure how it works, but if Muslim men die honorably (to them that is!), they are rewarded with 72 virgins. What do Muslim women get if they do the same? 72 virgin males?"*

Answer: *"Probably women in general might not enjoy 72 males in Paradise. We must realize that the likes of men versus women are quite different. Men generally desire women, while women are far more diverse in their desires. Women's nature is to have only one husband, so the women in Paradise will not wish for multiple husbands, and they will not be jealous to complain about their husbands having more than one wife.*

Assuming otherwise is belittling Allah's justice. As Muslims, we accept the reward that Allah will grant us in Paradise; we will be glad to have made it. Those who don't work for Paradise in this world will always complain and belittle what Allah will grant believers."

Bullshitto interpretation:

"You'll be lucky if Allah gives you anything, you ungrateful bitch, so if I were you, I'd shut my mouth and stop complaining about my husband having multiple wives in heaven and get down and ask for forgiveness for your attitude of entitlement!"

It would certainly be unfair of Allah to treat believers and nonbelievers the same. The fire of hell awaits those who reject Allah or cause mischief on earth (military conquest for the one true God, we're sure, doesn't qualify as mischief). Some of the punishments of hell are scorched skins that are continually changed out so you can feel the torment again, drinking 'festering' waters, having boiling water poured over your head, melting your insides as well as your skin, and hooks of iron to drag you back if you try to escape. Not exactly Club Med.

We found an interesting fun fact about hell that is apparently from one of the 'commentary' texts called Hadiths. These are believed to be a record of the words and actions of Muhammad as transmitted through chains of narrators. This one says that Muhammad saw that the majority of people in hell were women.

The Prophet said: *"I was shown the Hell-fire and that the majority of its dwellers were women who were ungrateful."*

It was asked: *"Do they disbelieve in Allah?"* (or are they ungrateful to Allah?)

He replied: *"They are ungrateful to their husbands and are ungrateful for the favors and the good (charitable deeds) done to them. If you have* *always been good (benevolent) to one of them and then she sees something in you (not of her liking), she will say, "I have never received any good from you."*

Sahih al-Bukhari 29 Vol. 1, Book 2, Hadith 29

From a marketing perspective, this is a shitty ad campaign unless it was featured in Patriarchy Today magazine; then it would probably sell like hotcakes. It sounds to us like the Prophet may have just had a bad day with one of his rebellious wives, but someone thought it was important enough to write it down.

As with all religions, there are different denominations within Islam, and they don't really agree with one another about the rules. Some are extremely harsh, while others have a softer, gentler rule system.

For instance, the penalty for adultery could be anything from 100 lashes to being stoned to death. While the Qur'an apparently doesn't specifically have a punishment for blasphemy, some more extreme sects see blasphemy as punishable by death, while the milder, gentler versions leave the punishment for such a thing to Allah and are taught to simply remove themselves from the company of blasphemers. So, the rules paint a broad stroke.

We guess they won't know who is correct in their interpretation of the rules until they get to Judgment Day and Allah either gifts them with a forever orgy or throws boiling water on them for eternity. It's a gamble for sure.

Our take on Islam from a marketing perspective is that we think the description of heaven is an easy sell to a male audience, but the path to get there and the rules that must be followed can be a bit much, depending on the denomination. Of course, the penalty of death for certain rule infractions is a powerful selling point all its own.

How this religion would have any appeal to women is a mystery, but then again, you can sell anything with a good marketing campaign.

JUDAISM

We would be remiss if we didn't include Judaism here because Christianity, Catholicism, and Islam all have their roots in the Jewish Torah (the first five books of the Bible, 'written' by Moses).

The Jewish faith is both simple and complicated. Perhaps it would be better to say that the beliefs are simple, but the rules are not.

Judaism is apparently the oldest Abrahamic monotheistic religion, meaning that its followers believe in the prophet Abraham as the cornerstone of the rest of the belief system.

As with the other religions based on Abraham, the Jews believe in one God; however, they do not believe God to be 'physical,' as is implied in other offshoot religions. They believe that God is a spiritual, whole, complete being that exists forever, is everywhere, and knows everything. God is above nature and the main power in the universe but still has time to record man's works and judge him accordingly.

On the surface, we like this definition of God because it sounds a lot like "Consciousness is all," which, is pretty close to what we'll be looking at later in the book. It goes awry when we get to the part about God expecting us to follow his laws or there will be retribution.

Judaism teaches that all people are made in the image of God; however, they also believe that God has no image, so not sure how we're making this leap. But because they believe that people are made in the image of God, they should be treated with dignity and respect. Again, this gets a little tricky when we get to the reward and retribution part.

In their view, goodness and morality come from God, and God is interested in what people do and watches them to make sure they're following the rules. God also gave man "free will," so you can do whatever you want, but you will be held accountable for your actions.

God rewards people who do 'good' and punishes those who do 'wrong.' Just on this fact alone, the whole 'made in the image of God' belief is nonsensical. God made humans in his image, and then sets them up for reward and punishment; however, this would necessarily mean that God would hold himself accountable as well and reward or punish himself. Kind of like an over-the-top perfectionist punishing themselves when they do something 'wrong'?

It's not clear how they make the leap from the Image of God to reward and punishment, but they don't have to be clear; that's the beauty of belief.

Similar to the Mormons, the Jewish hell is more of a 'spiritual washing machine' where your 'soul' gets cleansed of all your wrongdoings before you get to move on to their version of heaven. Their version of heaven is a little confusing, but as far as we can tell, heaven is like the Garden of Eden, where souls go after physical death to await the Messiah. Once the Messiah comes, everyone gets resurrected.

The good news is that the hell period for your soul only lasts a year. It isn't clear if everyone gets to move on to heaven after a year in hell or if the really bad guys get tortured forever or simply obliterated. The other question here is: what calendar are they using to mark a year? What if they're using the "a day is like a thousand years to God" calendar? We couldn't find the answer in the small print, and we think for a successful ad campaign, this should be disclosed so people can make an informed decision.

Wikipedia states that Jews believe they have a special job to repair the world. Their job is to make the world a better place by finding ways to lessen suffering and create peace and respect between people and protect the earth's environment from destruction. We aren't sure why God, who is everything, would need protection unless God is also the destruction, which would mean that their job is to protect God from himself. That's a little fucked up and a tall order.

They believe that the Messiah will come and unite the Jewish people and lead them in God's way; he will also unite the people of the world to serve God, and all people will act with justice and kindness. We'll finally have that 'world peace' that all the beauty pageant contestants long for. This is also apparently when the souls are bodily resurrected from heaven.

The rules required to be a good Jew and therefore go straight to heaven get super complicated and vary between sects in the Jewish religion. Their job is to bring peace and respect, but they can't even agree on the rules of their own religion. We suppose that's why the Messiah is necessary to unite them.

Their moral code is pretty basic: Embrace God's oneness, do not curse him, guard human life, respect animal life, respect the property of others, live a moral life, and ensure justice. Seems simple enough; however, 'live a moral life' and 'justice' are extremely vague and subjective terms, which is most likely why they have expanded the rules around these things.

The expanded rules are too lengthy and not important to go into here.

The biggest selling point of this religion, in our view, is that hell is limited to a year thing. It wouldn't be a good marketing move by itself; you would have to compare it side by side to other brands that offer eternal damnation, and then it becomes far more appealing.

BUDDHISM

Buddhism must be included in this section as it is also one of the largest world religions, with an estimated one billion followers. While on the surface it doesn't have as much in common with the others that we've examined, if we look closely enough, we may find that it has a similar underlying structure.

Buddhism is a non-theistic faith with no god or deity to worship; it is described as more of a philosophy or a moral code rather than an organized religion. But as much as it claims this, the sheer number of golden Buddha statues suggests that Buddha himself has been elevated to 'deity status,' the proverbial golden calf of the non-theistic faith.

It doesn't have the traditional heaven and hell ideologies of other religions, but it does have 'nirvana,' which is described as the highest state of profound well-being a human is capable of attaining. It is sold as liberation from suffering and ultimately liberation from the cycles of rebirth through extinguishing the fires of attachments, aversions, and ignorance in the mind.

Some call this state enlightenment. However, the very word enlightenment has been so misused and overused that it has now come to be synonymous with eternal bliss. We don't find this in the core of the Buddhist teachings, but we think that many of the people who fall for the modern Buddhist trap believe that's what they're buying.

As with all institutionalized belief systems, there are many varieties of Buddhism, and even they can't agree with each other. The Buddha Basics are listed here for context.

The Three Universal Truths:

1. Nothing in life is permanent and always changing.
2. Because nothing is permanent, a life based on possessing things or people doesn't make you happy.
3. There is no eternal, unchanging soul, and "self" is just a collection of changing characteristics or attributes.

The Four Noble Truths:

1. Human life has a lot of suffering.
2. The cause of suffering is desire.
3. There is an end to suffering.
4. The way to end suffering is to follow the middle path.

There is a laser-like focus on suffering. The human condition is suffering. The carrot being dangled is relief from suffering. Suffering may be the only word we have here, and it perhaps doesn't encapsulate the entire meaning; it may have a more subtle meaning, like dissatisfaction rather than outright suffering. Nevertheless, the idea is that human life is suffering, and you will keep suffering through endless cycles of rebirth until you 'get it.'

The good news is that you can find relief from suffering through many years of meditation and by following the teachings of the Eightfold Path. You might not make it to Nirvana in this lifetime; it may take several, but at least you've got a goal, and it's important to have goals.

There is also the idea that the ideal of Buddhist practice is to selflessly act to alleviate suffering wherever it appears. So, just as we see with other religions, this type of Buddhist practice focuses 'outward.' It deals with the 'appearance' of suffering external to 'you.' This is just a separation ideology.

The very concept of 'compassion' requires the suffering of yourself or others for it to be practiced. Compassion cannot exist without something to be compassionate about. So, we seek out suffering, generally outside of ourselves, never realizing that everything comes from within; then we practice "compassion" to ease the suffering.

The Eightfold Path:

- Right Understanding: Insight into the true nature of reality.
- Right Intention: The unselfish desire to realize enlightenment.
- Right Speech: Using speech compassionately.
- Right Action: Using ethical conduct to manifest compassion.
- Right Livelihood: Making a living through ethical and non-harmful means.
- Right Effort: Cultivating wholesome qualities and releasing unwholesome qualities.
- Right Mindfulness: Whole body and mind awareness.
- Right Concentration: Meditation or some other dedicated, concentrated practice.

This path is all based on the idea of separation. Who or what made the rulebook or the standard for what 'ethical' or 'wholesome' is? It's very subjective and alludes to something outside of you that you need to impress with your 'practice' to 'gain enlightenment' (unselfishly, of course).

It's hard to hate on Buddhism at its core; there are elements of truth in it. However, just like all the other religions, it has been bastardized through the ages so that it is now just a pop-culture pastime at worst and a lifelong circle jerk at the feet of a 'master' at best.

Buddhism isn't producing Buddhas. That alone should tell us that it got seriously messed up somewhere along the line. Most of the teachers are not enlightened, so what are they selling?

Buddhism has simply become another trumped-up reward/punishment system, just like all the other major religions, and it never quite delivers what it promises.

Buddhism has become a marketing marvel in the spiritual mall; every accoutrement that you can think of has some kind of Buddha logo: tea, herbs, beads, sand gardens, water fountains, artwork—you name it. It is no wonder that folks 'practice' for decades and still can't see the truth that is right in front of them.

Again, the simplest truth is hidden within the human need to complicate and mutilate it to conform to an assimilated matrix system.

BLIND BELIEF

We are looking at these belief systems to point out the commonalities and to open the door to questions.

Why are we so afraid of death that we have created all these stories about an afterlife? All the stories are rewards for belief and punishments for unbelief. It's frankly the Santa Claus story repackaged for adults.

These belief systems condition us to suffer through this life in hope of a glorious future in 'heaven.' This is the only life we have that we know of, and under these doctrines, we largely disregard this life in hope of a reward in the next one, which no one has ever proven exists. All of this is hearsay and wouldn't be allowed in a court of law, but we just blindly take it as the truth and waste the precious gift of life NOW in search of some fantasy in the future.

It's interesting that with all this 'belief' in the afterlife, the fear of death remains extremely strong. Perhaps there is that space inside each of us that knows that beliefs are not based in truth. If folks really, truly knew for sure that they were going to a paradise or heaven after they die, the fear of death wouldn't be present; it would be a welcome transition.

The only explanation for this is that either we suspect our beliefs are bullshit or we don't think we've done all the right things and may still be on the fence with the Almighty about our final destination. In fairness, there are people who do believe so strongly in their version of the fantasy that they are very willing to strap on a bomb and sacrifice themselves for their eternal reward.

For many, these religions and beliefs don't hold tremendous importance in their lives; they practice when convenient. They do the bare minimum to gain access to the big afterlife show; they only go to church on Easter or Christmas but still identify themselves with the chosen religion.

What's the point of that? You either believe or you don't. If you really believed, you would follow all the rules of your chosen faith and not just get a new outfit for the Easter service. True believers would adhere to all the rules, all the time, and get down and pray to the god of their choice on a regular basis, rather than just when the shit hits the fan.

True believers would base their entire lives on their faith; it would necessarily dictate how they vote, what products they support, and who they do business with. The world is full of folks who profess to believe, but when push comes to shove, it's generally only followed when convenient.

Here's the real issue: these beliefs are all based on so-called ancient texts. Jesus didn't write a book; in fact, what we consider the 'gospels' are not firsthand accounts but were written much later than when Jesus supposedly walked the earth. Further, we can't prove that Jesus existed at all, much less attribute words to him. If he did exist, he didn't teach Christianity as we know it today.

There is no proof that Buddha existed either; it's just commonly assumed that he did. If he did, he didn't write his own book; it was passed down orally through generations before it was written down. That alone should give us pause. It's like that old childhood game of 'telephone' where you whisper something to someone, and they whisper what they think they heard to the next person until you get to the end and that person has the message completely wrong.

Muhammad received some channeled messages from the angel Gabriel, Joseph Smith channeled Moroni, an angel no one has ever heard of, and yet much of the world's population blindly follows these hand-me-down ideas with absolutely no evidence that any of it is true. How did we come to this? Why does no one ask the important questions?

We would like to note that we have a special appreciation for the Bible, it's the one we are most familiar with; it tells you everything you need to know. It's a book about enlightenment when read with eyes to see and not read as a history book. That's the mistake. People take a book of texts that read more like a really great fantasy novel and claim it's actual history. Then we create all kinds of rituals that are necessary to please the God in the book.

The punishment for not believing is generally some kind of eternal damnation. No matter what religion you examine, they all have the same framework. Even if eternal damnation in a particular religion is just getting reincarnated for eternity until you work out your karma and get it right, it's still a reward/punishment system based on unproven theory.

What is constantly missed when looking at books like the Bible is that the books are not about ancient people. These books are about your story and your life—your own 'hero's journey.' When we miss this point, we get the institutional religion that we see today.

Religions are made by men. They wield great power over the masses. Some believe so sincerely in their version of the fairy tale that many are literally willing to die to defend it. Horrific wars are fought over whose version of the fantasy God is better, right, or true. Belief is a powerful thing and should be wielded with care.

All of our religious beliefs have been passed down from others: from teachers, preachers, priests, and gurus. We do not form our religions and beliefs on our own; we get them from someone else.

Do you see how these institutions, built solely on belief, take on an existence all of their own? They can't be questioned, and they believe in their own image of being a place of infallible truth. Nothing could be further from Truth than this, but that doesn't matter.

Have you ever wondered why our 'ancient' religious texts are so full of magic and miracles and all sorts of wondrous things, but we don't have those things today? Did the God(s) get bored with the whole talking-to-humans thing? Why no miracles now?

Jesus (supposedly) said in John 14:12, "...He that believeth on me, the works that I do shall he do also; and greater works than these shall he do; because I go to my Father."

No one is working miracles today. Do they just not believe hard enough? Perhaps the whole system isn't being taught correctly because, with the generations of true believers, we've not produced one who is doing greater works than Jesus.

Supposedly, a ninth-century Chinese Buddhist monk famously told his disciples, "If you meet the Buddha on the road, kill him."

This is along the same lines as doing greater works than Jesus. We're meant to go beyond the teacher, but no one does. When we meet the Buddha on the road, we stop, sit down, gaze lovingly at him, kiss his feet, and wait for his enlightenment to rub off on us. Buddhism isn't producing Buddhas; it is producing Buddhists.

Most religions stake the claim that their God is omnipresent. If they really understood this and believed it, then all of their teachings of separation, punishment and reward from the God outside of us would collapse like the house of cards that they are.

You can't have it both ways. God is either everywhere, all the time, or not. If their God is truly omnipresent, then that necessarily means that God is within everything and everyone, all the time. God would be the very substance that all things are made of, including us.

How could the omnipresent stuff that all things are made of even conceive of a reward for belief and a punishment for unbelief? It's nonsensical. Truth is often so simple that we can't see it.

We are up to our eyeballs in religions and belief systems, and not many people ever really question where they come from or if they have any basis in truth. We fall for every Tom, Dick, and Harry who speaks with supposed authority about a magical afterlife, and we willingly limit and hobble our lives that we are aware of *NOW* for a shot at the golden ticket in some distant future. We do this because of fear.

Fear is the basis of all religious beliefs. Religions are all fear wrapped up in priestly robes and rituals, passing themselves off as love.

There are many other religions in the world, and if we didn't cover one, it isn't because they are any better. It's because the result would be exactly the same. When we dissect these things properly, without all the fear and distortion, they all have the same underlying structure: reward and punishment and the requirement of belief to hold them up. It's that simple.

Now that we've covered the most popular death cults, let's transition into some more modern belief systems.

ARCHANGELS

Archangels are an interesting subject here because we find them in the major religions but also in the New Age Spirituality Marketplace. As we've seen, angels are responsible for the 'channeling' of both the Qur'an and the Book of Mormon. In New Age Nonsense, they've taken on an even bigger role. While the major religions have discounted any further 'channeling' because their books are complete, the Archangels in the New Age marketplace talk to just about everyone.

Let's just take the Archangel Michael. This guy is like the water cooler Archangel, standing around talking to anyone who will listen. Just do a quick internet search on Archangel Michael messages and boom! This guy is everywhere! There are several websites dedicated to telling us his messages, which generally start with 'Dear Ones,' a little condescending, but hey, he's an Archangel, right?

We are told on several websites dedicated to him that Michael is the chief Archangel and works constantly to protect us, has an aura of royal purple and royal blue with sparkles of gold. So, he's fancy. The fascination with Michael is almost a religion all its own.

We find him in the Bible, and interestingly, he's the only one with the title of Archangel. He supposedly only said four words in the entire Bible. In Jude 9, he says to Satan, "The Lord rebuke you!" This would imply that, though the belief is that he protects folks, he can't actually do anything to Satan; he has to call his dad to rebuke Satan. Maybe the reason Michael talks to everyone now is that he was pretty much edited out of the Bible, only getting the four words to his credit. Perhaps he feels cheated out of his 15 minutes of fame and is working tirelessly to right that wrong.

In the Catholic tradition, Michael has a few jobs: Leader of the Army of God, Angel of Death, Weigher of Souls, and Guardian of the Church. With all those titles, it's baffling how he has so much time to be the water cooler chatterbox.

After all these years, Michael apparently has much to say to humanity. We generally find him these days in the Ascension Super Store, with some crossover into the Galactic Federation, who are tirelessly fighting the dark ones trying to sabotage Earth's Ascension.

So how do we communicate with Michael?

We found this little list of eleven ways to communicate with Michael:

- Prayer
- Meditation
- Visualization
- Carry or wear a symbol, such as a pendant or charm with the sigil of Archangel Michael *(sold under an affiliate link, batteries not included)*
- Use specific crystals associated with Michael
- Light a blue candle
- Dreamwork
- Say a dedicated chant or mantra.

- Create a dedicated space decorated with symbols, candles, and crystals *(all sold here under an affiliate link)*
- Ask for signs
- Use oracle cards or other divination tools
- *(also sold under an affiliate link)*

We cannot verify that Michael has approved the "sigil" or anything else here, as he didn't respond to our request for an interview. Perhaps our candle wasn't 'blue enough' for him to come talk to us; it's hard to know. A quick trademark search on the sigil didn't reveal any further data, and we couldn't find Michael listed as the trademark owner, so our knowledge is limited. We also wanted to ask if Michael gets a cut from the affiliate link sales.

This fascination with Archangels is baffling to us. First of all, the Archangels are in the *lowest* order of angels according to the ranking done in the 5th or 6th century by Pseudo-Dionysius the Areopagite. He puts the order like this:

Highest: Seraphim, Cherubim, and Ophanim.

Middle: Dominions, Virtues, and Powers.

Lowest: Principalities, Archangels, and just plain old, run-of-the-mill angels.

One would think we would wish to hear from the *Highest* Order of Angels. But this may also explain Michael's need to prove himself by talking to anyone who will listen. He may be trying to work his way up to impress his superiors; we can all identify with that.

In fairness, we feel that we should mention the other Archangels as

THE SACRED ART OF SELF-DECEPTION

well; they too apparently speak to humanity; they just aren't as popular as Michael.

Here is what we could find on the seven main Archangels, their names, and meanings:

Michael: The name means "He who is as God." His role is to bring protection.

Raphael: The name means "God Heals." Responsible for healing physical and mental ailments. *(sounds to us like this is the guy people should be talking to)*

Gabriel: The name means "God is my strength." He is God's messenger.

Jophiel: The name means "Beauty of God." Responsible for guiding you to see the beauty in all things.

Ariel: The name means "Lion of God." Responsible for protecting the earth and its resources and inhabitants.

Azrael: The name means "Whom God helps." Responsible for helping the dead transition to the spirit realm (Angel of Death).

Chamuel: The name means "He who sees God." Responsible for bringing peace to the world.

We aren't sure these guys are really performing at their top level, especially Chamuel; his job is the toughest for sure, but we aren't seeing peace in the world and haven't since the beginning of recorded history. Also, if Gabriel is the communicator, why does Michael do most of the talking? The current state of both physical and mental well-being in society would also suggest that Raphael isn't qualified for his job either.

Who is in charge of these guys?

Shouldn't the CEO come in and clean house if they aren't performing?

How many times have they been written up in their angelic employee file?

How can the angelic organization run efficiently when these guys have been underperforming all this time?

Perhaps this is why our world is in such disarray; those tasked with helping the earth are miserable failures.

NEW AGE SPIRITUALITY

New Age Spirituality has the traditional religions to thank for its existence.

Without those big box stores, no one would come to the mall. The New Age folks took some of the basic concepts of traditional religion and made their version of 'heaven' so fucking wonderful that it appears to be sprinkled with unicorn dust and sparkly sequins, and you would have to be an idiot not to want it. It's a far more appealing package, and folks are rushing into these stores to buy it.

These stores come in all shapes and sizes; there's something for everyone! Let's take a look at some of the fantastic things we can find in the New Age product lines.

MANIFESTING

The Manifesters are some of our favorites. You can't throw a rock without hitting some kind of "Manifest the Life of Your Dreams" program, seminar, workshop, or certification these days. Everyone goes for this. The sheer multitude of courses offered that make you a "Certified Manifester" is stunning. You pay your fee and manifest a certificate; the course creator manifests the money. See how that works? If all these folks were Master Manifesters, why charge the fee at all?

The Law of Attraction has become incredibly popular in recent years. The popularity stems from what our Buddhist friends would call dissatisfaction. We find that folks are mostly interested in easing the dissatisfaction with their lives due to their belief in lack. Not many people really want to do the work to figure out why the lack of something is there in the first place; we just want a magic pill to make it all better.

It's a little heartbreaking from our point of view. Don't misunderstand; manifesting is a wondrous thing. What's heartbreaking is that the way it's taught misses the most important point. Your perceived reality from the ego-character identified point of view is simply reflecting the 'you' that you think you are, back to you.

We also find the constant focus on positive thoughts and emotions to be incorrect and limiting. The reward/punishment paradigm is interwoven in the 'manifesting' ideology that is currently peddled to the masses. It is based on separation, and so the way this subject is currently sold to the seeker is false.

The Law of Attraction is sold as a 'spiritual law.' The term "law" makes it sound authoritative. These teachings are not laws; in fact, they are incorrect. They are based on the premise that the "universe" is something 'out there' that responds to you as a separate entity from itself. Your job is to have only positive thoughts, say some affirmations, and bam! You have the life of your dreams.

If we hold this up to the light of the Truth of one, as in there is only one thing, (we're calling it consciousness in this book), it is immediately apparent that this is simply another carrot for you to chase but never catch. From the perspective of oneness, who would be attracting what? Where would they be attracting it from? Further, as we'll see later in this book, focusing solely on positive versus negative thoughts is a limiting experience. It also comes with its own reward and punishment system. The universe gives to those who think happy thoughts and withholds from those who don't.

If you are one of the millions of people who have spent loads of money on these types of teachings and have nothing to show for it but a desire to buy more books and courses, please read on. There is a reason this doesn't work.

To create something different, you actually need to understand the core concept of who and what you are and work there first. But most people don't really want to do any kind of serious work or self-discovery. We just want to manifest a million bucks and a smoking-hot significant other. No one really wants to wake up and get out of the dungeon; we just want to redecorate the cell.

NEW AGE CELEBRITIES

Another of our most popular stores in the mall is where we find the New Age Celebrities. They've been on this circuit for years and have made a booming business out of it. Masses of people go to their seminars and workshops, paying $1,500 for the cheap seats and up to $10,000 for the VIP tickets.

We're always amazed by this. Do you become more awake if you're in the VIP seats? Does the magical awakening happen faster, or is it more intense if you're in closer proximity to the star of the show?

These seminars and retreats are well thought out, using just the right music to get you pumped up and put you in a state of suggestibility for the ultimate 'mass hypnotic' type vibe and pampering that takes place. At some point, you may witness and even participate in superhuman feats, and you go home so full of confidence that you finally 'have it' and can do anything! Your life will never be the same!

This generally lasts about three weeks, and then you're right back in the same place you were before. The problem is that now you have this amazing memory of a spiritual high or mystical experience so awesome that you'll now spend enormous amounts of time and money to chase it. So, you keep showing up to more and more seminars and workshops, trying to get that feeling again.

You just KNOW that one more time will make it stick.

It is not in their best interest for you to leave these seminars with verifiable, lasting change. A one-and-done personal development seminar is not a sustainable business model. You need to ask yourself, do they actually have the product they are selling, and if they do, why doesn't it work the first time?

One of the clues is in the term 'personal development.' It's not marketed as a 'personal best attainment' seminar; it is rightfully marketed as personal development, meaning that it must continue to be developed; it can never be achieved. So, we keep going back to get more and more 'developed,' thinking that we are on our way to finally being the person we need to be.

You ARE capable of amazing feats; that's not false. The point we're making is that while some of these things are based on something real, to make lasting change, you must get to the core concept of who and what you are, and that's what's lacking with these types of programs.

The reasons they leave this vital part out may be that they don't have it themselves and so they can't teach it, or they understand that once you discover who you really are, you won't require the seminars any longer, and they'll be out of a gig.

CONSCIOUS LIVING

At the time of this writing, there is an 'expo' going on in a couple of months in Los Angeles. It's the 22nd annual expo for 'conscious living.' To give you an example of the absolute absurdity of where our 'spiritual mall' is, we'll just give you a few examples of the workshops on the schedule: (Bear with us; the list is a little long. Don't skim over it; really read this with intention and clarity.)

- UFO Reporting and Human Evolution
- 5D Soul Mission Activation
- Star-Fleet: Gamifying
- Planetary Transformation
- Galactic Star Code Activation
- Kathara Grid Star Gate Activation
- What Does Living in 5D Really Mean?
- Earth's Ascendancy & Cosmic Consciousness
- Working with Divine Light Beings
- Detox to Open Your Third Eye
- Initiation of Cosmic Dragons
- Galactic Light Language for Ascension
- Activate Your Starseed Mission
- Angel Communication Using Spiritual Law
- Realize Your Divine Potential
- Dragon K-Ryu Activation
- Cats Are Starseeds and Ascension Guides
- A Community Model for the New Earth

Yes, these are real workshops, and yes, our response was something along the lines of, "You have got to be fucking kidding me."

These are just a few of the wondrous offerings of the 'spiritual mall.' When you look at them all together, it becomes laughable.

How many 'activations' does one need? How did all the Galactic/Starfleet ideas become synonymous with 'conscious living'? When did they slide in and cuddle up to spirituality?

As we understand it, the Galactic Federation is hovering above and observing the 'Earthling Truman Show,' but they are not allowed to interfere with our little Earth show. They're just supposed to be on standby to be our saviors if the human self-destructive tendencies go a little too far.

But now they're communicating with tons of people and handing out these 'activations' like Oprah hands out cars. "YOU get an activation! And YOU get an activation! Activations for Everyone!" Isn't that kind of interfering with the show?

LIGHTWORKERS

The Lightworkers or Lightwarriors, as some call themselves, have become quite popular over the last few years as well. Just what is a Lightworker? We're glad you asked!

According to one website we found, "Lightworkers are high vibrational spirits that drive themselves and others around them forward. They commit themselves to serving others with love and compassion, and, if you're reading this, you might well be one."

WHAAAAT?! We might be Lightworkers?

Though you can't scroll through social media without running into a Lightworker of some sort, this Lightworker website says that they are complicated, misunderstood, and incredibly rare. They do offer a test that you can take to ascertain if you are one of those incredibly rare vibrational spirits. We decided to take the quick online quiz because, I mean, we found our way to the website, and it wouldn't be right to just ignore the possibility that we might be Lightworkers and have some kind of mission.

The quiz does come with a warning that it is entirely possible for the quiz to turn up negative. Not everyone is a Lightworker, but the fact that we are spiritually aware enough to know of their existence is a great start.

Our result from the quiz was......... Wait for it..........

> "Your Results are.... RARE. Your combination of answers is certainly interesting. I don't just want to tell you what you are – I'd like to help guide you on your spiritual path ahead. Tell me where I can get in touch with you, and I'll start with a blueprint on your spiritual development. (I won't share your email with anyone else)."

We're sorry to report, we did not get an email with our Lightworker score, so now we are left in the dark and will never know if we have a mission to save humanity.

There are apparently different kinds of Lightworkers:

The Gatekeeper Lightworker, also known as the protector or Gridworker. They protect normal people in the physical realm from the negative entities in the other lower dimensions.

The Healer Lightworker. These are the most empathic, and they're here to heal humanity as a whole.

The Wayshower Lightworker guides other lost souls when they get lost on their path.

The Transmuter Lightworker is here to transmute light for the light beings in the universe. They help light from other dimensions come into this world and transform dark areas.

The Oracle Lightworker is here to help Lightworkers and light beings communicate better.

The Lightkeeper Lightworker is the spiritual anchor for everyone around them.

There are many more types of Lightworkers, and this is apparently just scratching the surface of what Lightworkers do, but it would appear that we have them to thank for the very survival of humanity!

Let's look at some of the signs that you may be a Lightworker:

- Your young life was set up for a series of traumas, challenges, and other difficulties. *(Childhood trauma)*
- You are constantly on a mission to improve your own life and the lives of those around you; you are driven to 'fix' things for others. *(People pleasing and co-dependence)*
- Though you once may have struggled with certain mental illnesses, you have come to understand that they were adaptations to your circumstances rather than innate problems. *(Mental illness, a valuable tool)*
- You feel that you don't belong or fit in anywhere. *(Identity crisis)*
- You intuitively know that you are alive for a higher purpose. *(Man's search for meaning)*
- You are empathic and highly sensitive to others' energies. *(Poor boundaries)*

These are just a few of the 'signs' that you may be a Lightworker. It is not an exhaustive list, and certainly, these signs don't guarantee that you are a Lightworker. If you are a Lightworker, though, we aren't sure what your job is.

What do Lightworkers do, how do they do it, and what is the point? Is there an apprenticeship program? We're sure a quick internet search would reveal many sites and organizations ready to take your money to train you to be a 'Lightworker.'

How did this nonsense even become a 'thing'? Just a quick internet search on 'Lightworkers' and you'll find hundreds, if not thousands, of posts about the

"21 signs you're a Lightworker," "How to become a Lightworker," "Are you a Lightworker?" and "What kind of Lightworker are you?"

There is absolutely no evidence of any kind, anywhere, that there is such a thing as a Lightworker, let alone the astral planes, dark entities, light beings, or the 'other side.' No evidence at all for any of it.

The term "Lightworker" was coined by Michael Mirdad in the early '80s and then made popular by Doreen Virtue in 1997, and bam!

Instead of just being those people who do too much for others and don't properly take care of themselves and don't have proper boundaries, they've made it into a good thing.

They've now made this into something to be revered as a special mission, special gift, and special talent; and instead of getting to the bottom of their bullshit about their trauma, codependency, and need to earn their worth, they just decide they're on a special mission to save humanity.

This is one of the mind's most masterful delusions—masking anxiety, trauma response, depression, and energetic sensitivity as some kind of inter-dimensional superhero responsible for the survival of the human race. Fucking amazing.

STARSEEDS

The concept of Starseeds has become increasingly popular in the last fifteen years or so. The concept comes to us again from channelers. According to these channelers, most agree that Starseeds are traveling souls from other planets who incarnated on Earth to inspire and heal human beings and to participate in the planet's evolution. They are individuals said to be born from stardust and infused with a divine light.

Signs you may be a Starseed:

- You feel like you don't belong *(said every teenager, at some point)*.
- You're very intuitive and psychic.
- You're so empathic that it can be crippling *(or social anxiety)*.
- You are an 'old soul' *(assuming souls exist, which can't be proven)*.
- You don't bond deeply with others. *(as with abandonment issues and trauma response)*.
- You see repeating numbers.
- You have unexplainable physical ailments that doctors cannot pinpoint (extreme fatigue, heart palpitations, tingling in your hands and feet, memory lapses, anxiety, and headaches to name a few).

If you're a Starseed, these symptoms will be related to your chakras opening; if you are NOT a Starseed, you should get medical attention. Interestingly, these symptoms also match high cortisol or high histamine, and just popping an antihistamine or some Ashwagandha might make it all better.

Chakra opening is a lot sexier, though. This is NOT medical advice.

SHADOW EASTON & LUCAS EASTON

SHADOW IS THINKING OUT LOUD:

"Starseeds???"

"If there are Starseeds do we have Sunseeds?"

"Never heard of Sunseeds."

"Hm... are there Sunseeds?"

"Why aren't there any Sunseeds?"

SHADOW ASKS:

"Babe!"

"Have you found anything relating to Sunseeds in any of your research for the book?"

LUCAS RESPONDS:

"Sunseeds?"

"Hmm?"

"Nope, I don't think anyone is claiming to be a Sunseed, not that I can find. Which seems weird. Seems like if the Sun is the biggest star, they would be even more powerful souls, right?"

SHADOW REPLIES:

"Yeah, that's kind of where my thoughts were going."

THE SACRED ART OF SELF-DECEPTION

LUCAS SAYS:

"I don't think anyone is doing Sunseeds, is that a niche market?"

"I mean, the marketing possibilities are amazing."

SHADOW REPEATS THE WORD OVER AGAIN:

"Sunseeds, Sunseeds, Sunseeds…"

"Kind of sounds like a snack."

LUCAS AGREES:

"It IS a great name for a snack!"

"This is a million-dollar idea if you do it right."

SHADOW ASKS:

"Where would we start?"

LUCAS THINKS FOR A MINUTE AND REPLIES:

"Well, first, we would need a logo."

"Let me see what I can come up with."

"…"

A FEW HOURS LATER…

SUNSEEDS

SHADOW EXCLAIMS:

"Oh my gosh, I love it!"

LUCAS SMILES AND SAYS:

"I think our first product is really just the raw seeds."

"Have to start somewhere, right?"

…

SUNSEEDS Originals

SUNSEEDS - "Certified organic, gluten-free, no preservatives or additives, vegan and keto approved, and no animal testing. Certified by the Buddha Compassionate Heart Society as a 'living food' to fuel your enlightenment!"

SUNSEEDS - "Energizing light bodies since 1979!"

SUNSEEDS - "We bring good things to Light…. Bodies."

SUNSEEDS – "NOW as **SUNSEEDS Light**! Half the kilowatts, all the illumination!"

COMMERCIAL:

"Did you fail to walk on hot coals at the last personal development seminar you attended? There's a **SUNSEED** for that!"

"Taking your **SUNSEEDS** daily will have you making those hot coals your bitch and manifesting your ass off in three weeks or your money back!"

SADOW SAYS:

"That is great babe!"

"Looks fantastic."

LUCAS REPLIES:

"It's a good start."

"But I feel like some sort of snack bar would be great."

"Something you can take with you."

…

SUNSEEDS Energy Bar

SUNSEEDS Ascension Crunch – "For your 5D Go Bag! Don't leave 3D without them!"

"Fast track your timeline shift with **SUNSEEDS Ascension Crunch**, the official snack of the Galactic Federation!"

SUNSEEDS Ascension Crunch – "Now available at every rest stop on the galactic highway!"

COMMERCIAL:

"Don't let your light body dim on the way to Ascension: keep it glowing with **SUNSEEDS Ascension Crunch!**"

SHADOW IS OVER THE MOON:

"It's SO GOOD!"

"I think we can expand on this idea."

"What about energy drinks? People love those!"

LUCAS THINKS ABOUT IT:

"Hmmm… SUNSEEDS in liquid form?"

"Yeah, I think that would be perfect."

…

THE SACRED ART OF SELF-DECEPTION

SUNSEEDS Energy Drink

SUNSEEDS - "Now in liquid form! Able to withstand quantum timeline jumping!"

SUNSEEDS Liquid - "Fuel Your Frequency!"

SUNSEEDS Liquid – "Now available in the **NEW** TO GO Pouch!"

COMMERCIAL:

SUNSEEDS Liquid Solar Burn. "Scientifically proven to burn your carbon body 5 times faster."

"Get that summer light body you've been dreaming of with **SUNSEEDS Liquid Solar Burn!**"

LUCAS IS REALLY GETTING INTO THE GROOVE NOW:

"Hey, what about supplements?"

"Like something for kids, maybe?"

"What do you think?"

SHADOW REPLIES:

"Yes, absolutely!"

"I think that parents would love that."

...

SUNSEEDS Gummies

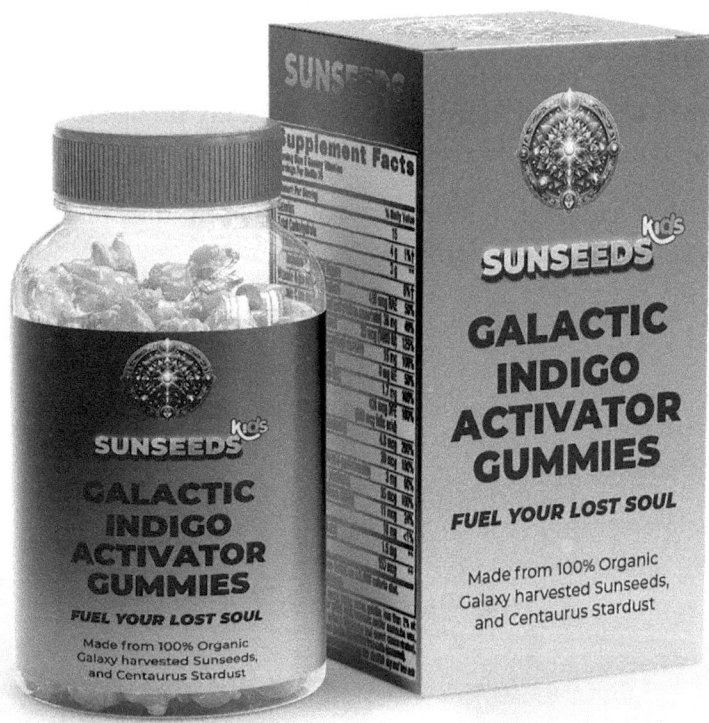

SUNSEEDS Gummies - "Activating Indigo Children since 1985."

SUNSEEDS Gummies - "Now in pill form!"

COMMERCIAL:

"Are you worried that your child is not an Indigo child?"

"Are you embarrassed by their lack of a humanity-saving galactic mission?"

"Do you think they aren't living up to their potential?"

"Try **SUNSEEDS Gummies** and watch your pathetic earth child transform into the Galactic Superhero they were born to be!"

NOW SHADOW IS GETTING EXCITED AND SHE STARTS THINKING ABOUT OTHER TYPES OF PRODUCTS:

"Hey, what about beauty products?"

"Women love it and they are the majority in the Spiritual Marketplace."

LUCAS AGREES:

"Yes. That is a big market."

"..."

SUNSEEDS Pristine

SUNSEEDS Pristine – "Get the wrinkle-free light body you deserve."

SUNSEEDS Pristine – "Your 3rd Eye will open so wide you will need two pairs of sunglasses."

SUNSEEDS Pristine R. – "Reiki-infused **SUNSEEDS** for your healing journey!"

LUCAS IS ALL IN:

"I think there would be a market for older people as well."

"Don't you think?"

SHADOW AGREES:

"Sure."

"I mean the geriatric market is huge!"

"Just look at the amount of Senior Living Places."

"We could set up direct distribution and monthly subscriptions."

LUCAS REPLIES:

"Oh, I like the way you are thinking."

...

SUNSEEDS Silver

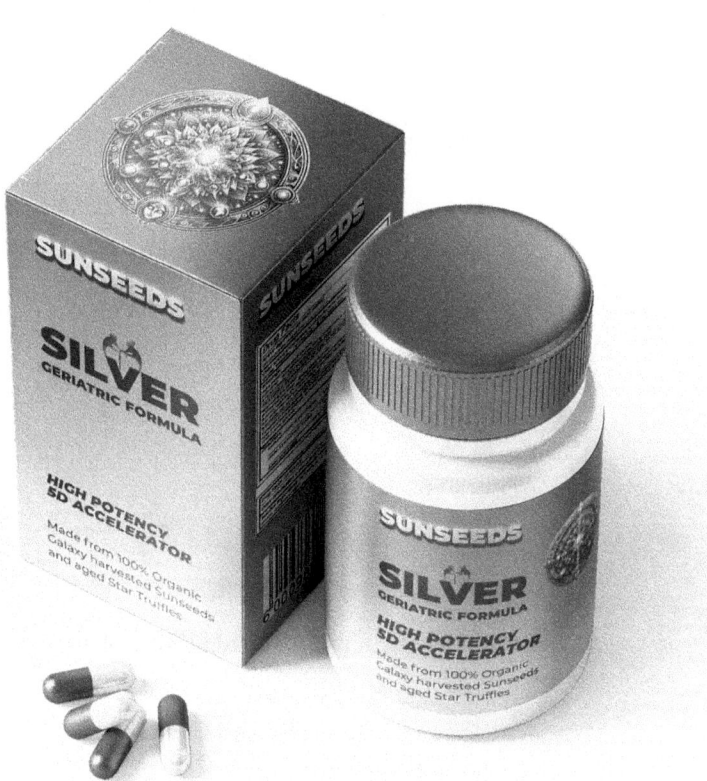

SUNSEEDS Silver – "NOW available as suppositories. Bringing light to the darkest places."

SUNSEEDS SILVER Suppositories - "Illumination where the sun don't shine!"

COMMERCIAL:

"Exhausted waiting for your ascension for the last 50 years?"

"Try **SUNSEEDS Silver**, specially formulated for the geriatric lightworker!"

Both Shadow and Lucas are laughing uncontrollably.

> SHADOW CATCHES HER BREATH AND ASKS:
> "Do you think we're taking this too far?"

> LUCAS REPLIES:
> "Fuck no!"
> "This is awesome!"
> "I think that's enough products but now we have to think about how we're going to get the word out. Like social media, website with SEO, maybe partnerships or sponsorships, and endorsements, that stuff can really blow a brand up."
> ...

THE SACRED ART OF SELF-DECEPTION

SUNSEEDS Partnerships / Endorsements / Sponsorship

SUNSEEDS - "Proud sponsor of the **Pleiadian Formula 5D Racing Team.**"

SUNSEEDS - "Ascension Booster. Proudly endorsed by Archangel Michael!"

SUNSEEDS - "Official sponsor of the **Galactic Illumination Awards!**"

SUNSEEDS AstralGlide - "The official lubrication of **GAAPS** (Grey Alien Anal Probe Society)."

(Suitable for both carbon and light bodies for vaginal or anal use. If itching and burning should occur, consult your metaphysician.)

www.sunseeds.life - Your galactic one stop shop to fuel your frequency.

LUCAS ADDS:

"Then we need to think about press releases."

"That's really helpful with back-linking and Search Engine Optimization."

...

THE SACRED ART OF SELF-DECEPTION

SUNSEEDS Announcements / Press Releases

ORION COMMUNITY NEWS

"SUNSEEDS.LIFE SECURES EXCLUSIVE NAMING RIGHTS TO THE GALACTIC FEDERATION SPORTS ARENA..."

The New SUNSEEDS Stadium

Experts all over the Universe agree and are calling it the contract of the millenium. For an undisclosed sum SUNSEEDS secured the rights to

Unions cause Earth Ascension delay

Due to the ongoing strike of Light-workers, Light-Warriors and the Starseed Union the estimated time frame for Earths Ascension has now

For Immediate Release: "Sunseeds.life secures the exclusive rights to the **Galactic Federation Sports Arena**."

For Immediate Release: "**Galactic Federation** endorses **SUNSEEDS** as the official snack of the **Lightbody Olympics!**"

For Immediate Release: "**Catholic Church** endorses **SUNSEEDS** for use in holy communion for faster absorption of the body of Christ."

SHADOW EXCLAIMS:

"Holy Shit!"

"I think we've really got something here!"

"This will be big."

LUCAS AGREES, SMILING:

"Yep, 100%."

"I'll work on this a little more this week."

"I want to make sure we have everything ready to go."

"Need to get the website and online store up and running."

"Still have to tie in the Payment Gateway and test everything."

…

THE SACRED ART OF SELF-DECEPTION

www.sunseed.life

AS SEEN ON

ENTER PROMO CODE
"AWAKE"
FOR
25% OFF

WITH EVERY PURCHASE OF SUNSEEDS, A PORTION OF THE PROFITS ARE DONATED TO THE

Shadow remembers what she's supposed to be doing:

"Oh shit!"

"What happened?"

"Guess we got a bit sidetracked here."

"So where were we?"

"Yes ... Sunseeds."

...

"No, no ... wait."

...

"STARSEEDS."

"Yes, Starseeds."

...

"OK."

...

"Let's continue."

There are apparently different types of Starseeds, much like there are different types of Lightworkers. We find a lot of overlap between the two lists of 'how to know you are one.'

We'll take a look at a few of the types of Starseeds here from one of the many websites we found.

Pleiadian:

Origin Realm: Star cluster Pleiades – in the Taurus constellation.

Features: Typically tall, slim, and long-limbed with blond hair and blue eyes.

Mission: To record Earth's history.

This is apparently a matriarchal society that exalts relationships, family, children, and women. Divine Feminine energy is recognized as a powerful frequency to harness creation and love.

Bullshitto commentary:

So, just as we see with patriarchal beliefs and societies, this would suggest that the Pleiadians are extremely unbalanced as a society leaning heavily toward the 'feminine' and we aren't sure taking advice from them would be wise.

Sirian:

Origin Realm: Planets Sirius A and B in Vega, in the Lyra constellation.

Features: Lion-like appearance but attracted to canines. *(What the actual F does that mean?)*

Mission: To save the planet.

The Sirians are said to have a strong, grounded connection to the Earth. They are level-headed and logical in their thinking; they love all canines but have a feline appearance and tendencies.

Ascended masters, like Jesus and other holy figures, are believed to be of this Starseed.

Bullshitto Commentary:

WHAAAAATTT?! Jesus looked like a cat and had cat tendencies but loved dogs? What are feline tendencies? Did he give himself tongue baths? Chase mice?

Was he able to leap amazingly high from a standing position?

Did he have nine lives? That would kind of suck for Jesus: I mean, if they all ended like the first one.

Imagine doing THAT nine times.

Arcturian:

Origin Realm: Star Arcturus in the Boötes Constellation.

Features: Darker complexion; low body temperature and low blood pressure.

Mission: To bring spiritual healing and grounding to humans while on Earth.

Arcturians are said to have reached the pinnacle of emotional and mental advancement so that they act as shamans and healers to bring awareness of the spiritual in our physical reality.

They actually live in the fifth dimension in a divine realm where souls leaving Earth pass through the Arcturian energetic field to recenter before they rebirth in another realm or back on Earth.

Bullshitto Commentary:

Seriously? Reincarnation with a slightly different twist? That's the best they could do with all that emotional and mental advancement, reimagining reincarnation? Disappointing.

Indigo, Crystal & Rainbow:

Origin Realm: Earth's spiritual dimension.

Features: Diverse.

Mission: To serve humans selflessly in pursuit of consciousness.

Indigos and Crystals have specially endowed powers—from Archangel Michael and Archangel Gabriel, respectively. Indigos work for justice and peace and have no tolerance for unfairness or evil. Crystals bring joy, light, and harmony in thought and action to balance the raging spirit of Indigos.

Rainbows are the youngest wave of healing frequency on Earth, and we are still coming to understand their spiritual role. That's why many Rainbows seem detached from humans.

However, all three understand this detachment from the physical. Their work on Earth serves to strengthen their spiritual resolve for future reincarnations.

Bullshitto Commentary:

We included this one just for the Archangel reference. The Archangels are now specially endowing powers rather than just having a chat at the water cooler. We do need to point out the obvious here: Rainbows are the 'youngest' and seem detached from other humans. This sounds incredibly similar to the autism spectrum, and that would explain a lot.

The lengths that we will go to make ourselves feel special are absolutely mind-blowing. This Starseed thing is like the Lightworker thing on steroids. We have a community of people who think they "don't belong," are disconnected, and don't bond well with others, who have fabricated the reason for these things to be that they are not of human origin.

Again, they have a savior complex and a special mission to save humanity or fight the darkness. The mind is a masterful storyteller.

When did we all become Starseeds and Lightworkers? This was kind of a slow burn, we think. Years ago, these folks were outliers. Today, we see this everywhere. Content with the term #starseed has over one billion views on TikTok alone.

Light Language seems to be the new kid on the block these days. Having had some exposure to the Pentecostal church, this makes sense to us. It's the same idea as speaking in tongues. The same theory applies: gibberish that no one can interpret, but it gets us all hyped up for heaven/ascension.

Light Language apparently came from the Starseeds. They believe it bypasses human limitations and is the language of the soul.

These Lightworker, Starseed, and Light Language beliefs are exactly why we now have the term 'spiritual psychosis.'

Imagine how much energy these folks put into this nonsense. And for what? What is the end goal here? We don't think there is one.

It's just another carrot-chasing system to keep people in some kind of spiritual search but never getting them anywhere. The satisfaction is in the searching; it never had anything to do with finding.

This is just more of the savior dynamic but with a lot more pampering.

Everyone gets to be special, and everyone gets to ascend, but some of us were placed here with a secret mission to *help* everyone else ascend.

So, to all you light warriors battling the dark forces and guarding the earth's energy grids so we can all transition into the New World, we say thank you for your service. We raise our glasses in a toast to you with a shot of pure illumination: Liquid Sunseeds.

The things we've looked at here may sound like outliers in the spiritual mall, but the Zen Masters, the secret teachings, and a lot of other more 'mainstream' offerings aren't any better if you're looking for truth. All these varying themes are simply the same idea of religion in a different costume.

There is something innately wrong with us; they all have some kind of savior solution, whether it's starships, destroying the Ego or only having positive thoughts.

They produce constant seekers, not finders. It's so damn mesmerizing to us, though; it's like the promise of heaven without all the hell stuff to counteract it. They are selling an image of 'Nirvana' or a 'New Earth' and we lap it up.

SOUL RECLAMATION

Social media is an amazing gold mine of spiritual nonsense. People are making serious money off our ignorance of who and what we are.

We had a friend who saw an ad on social media for a course called "Reclaim the Lost Parts of Your Soul." She was thinking of purchasing this course, and immediately our alarm bells went off.

We had several questions. We asked her, "How do they charge, by the number of lost soul parts, or is there an all-in option? Can you get your money back if you fail to reclaim all the lost parts of your soul? Is there a dashboard or something where you can accurately track how many lost parts have been reclaimed? Do you get a partial refund if some are reclaimed but not all? Do you get a discount or bonus points if most of your soul is already intact?"

This course sold for $2,500 all in—no matter how many lost parts you had. After this conversation, our friend did not purchase this course, but plenty of other people probably did, without asking any of these questions.

Where would the lost parts of the soul go? Where are they that they can't find their way back? Why didn't the other parts of the soul keep these parts intact? Is there a universal maze with little fragments of lost souls wandering around, waiting for some secret magic words to pull them back to us?

Not only are we separate from our soul, but our soul is separated from itself? That's a lot of separation and sounds like a hopeless situation. Who wouldn't pay a king's ransom to get their soul back?

'Soul' is another one of those words we use that we don't think about. First, it has not been, nor will it ever be, proven that a soul exists, and second, if it did, what exactly the soul would be. We all just assume that there is this 'soul' inside of us that is separate from who we are.

This idea has been around so long that we don't think to question it. But when we look at it with discernment, it's readily apparent that this idea of a soul separate from you is nonsense.

ASCENSION

The Ascension / 5D / Cosmic Consciousness folks are a personal favorite simply because of the absolute mental gymnastics that are required to make any of this make sense. It's fun to ask these folks serious questions and then watch them circle jerk around a word salad.

Here's an example we pulled from a website all about the Ascension process:

"Ascension in its simplest terms is altering consciousness from one level to another. In other words, ascension is the process of expanding beliefs that make up the base level of consciousness to the point that a new reality is manifest. Consciousness is, after all comprised of the beliefs, thoughts, actions, and choices that form the tapestry of reality. When consciousness expands, elevates, and changes, reality cannot help but change in response. Ascension is elevating consciousness into a new dimension of experience."

There is so much nonsense here that it would require an entire book to break this down. They use words like "consciousness" without telling you how they define it, and it's apparently subject to belief. From our perspective, no belief is true.

We'll talk more about this later in the book. Anything based purely IN belief and based ON separation, is untruth.

Let's take a look at the steps required for ascension from this same website.

Open your heart and consciously return to the vibration of love. *(How are we defining love? How would you return to it?)*

Spend over half your time lovingly serving and supporting others in a state that is free from judgment, expectation, and Ego-based attachment. Respect, serve, and honor all of life on Earth. Raise your vibration, purify your vessel, and activate your DNA. *(Sorry, what?)*

Awaken your Lightbody and reconnect with the light and vibration of your higher self. *(My Lightbody?)*

Meditate. *(On what?)*

Set the conscious intention to ascend. *(What does this even mean?)*

Choose your ascension and continue to take steps to raise your vibration, release fear, and connect with the blissful field of unified Source Consciousness. *(Unified Source Consciousness? What is that, exactly? Is there an Ununified Source Consciousness?)*

Now, if you're a frequent shopper in our new age mall, all of this will probably sound okay to you. We're using fun words like love, service to others, vibration, and Lightbody! This is all fluff and based on separation. Anything that must mention some kind of "Unified Source Consciousness" is based on separation. Separation is untrue.

Further, when did we ascertain that the Lightbody idea is true?

How are we using the word "love" here?

"Spend over half your time serving others" – so if you only spend a quarter of your time, your ascension dreams will never come true? So many questions!

The entire idea of ascending from 3D to 5D or beyond is just the Christian rapture repackaged. As far as we can find, this idea didn't come around until the 1970s, and it is likely tied to the idea of the "Age of Aquarius." In this ascension belief system, 3D is full of anger, fear, and pain, while 5D is all love, light, rainbows, and unicorns. To put it into more familiar terms, 3D is hell, and 5D is heaven.

The idea of Ascension has now branched off into several different variations. The most common turn that it has taken is it's now a 'war' between light and dark. There is a belief that everyone must raise their 'vibration' sufficiently high so that we can all 'ascend' to

5D together, and then there is also the belief in the dark forces trying to stop this ascension.

It's the same old good vs. evil storyline: God vs. Satan, or Luke Skywalker vs. Darth Vader. But now it's the Galactic Federation and the Archangels against the Reptilians or some such nonsense. It's just repurposed and repackaged for an increasingly misguided audience.

Some information we found on another website regarding this process says that ascension requires you to 'activate your DNA' so that you can power up your Lightbody. This same website states that the "Lightbody is an energy-based existence beyond the physical body. It is fueled by our constant ecstatic frequency of unconditional love. This is how we dissolve back into source and achieve immortality as it was promised." *(We assume that this promise is taken from the religious teaching about eternal life.)*

Again, it's just religion in a different package.

They even get science into the game. They point to the Schumann Resonances as proof that the earth's frequencies are rising. The Schumann Resonances are a set of spectrum peaks in the extremely low-frequency portion of the earth's magnetic field. You can see these charts online, and they are super important looking and colorful. The ascension folks have turned this into some kind of 'proof' of their theory.

There are millions of posts on social media at any given time showing the chart with comments like:

"Oh, look at the chart today! Did you feel the energy? I got so many downloads last night! We're getting soooo close! I'm exhausted and my body aches, must be ascension symptoms!"

Large groups of people are on these social media sites comparing their ascension symptoms. This is just looking for group validation, and as we'll see later, the placebo effect comes into play. If you have these 'ascension symptoms,' then you must be one of the chosen ones who is actually ascending; if you don't, your mind will create them to convince you that you too are ascending. What an amazing construct!

None of these folks actually understand the charts or electromagnetics, but they parade this out as proof of ascension.

Spoiler Alert: According to what we could find on the subject, the Schumann resonances are not rising. Resonances fluctuate, not rise or fall significantly. When you see the spikes on the charts, it's voltage spikes, not resonances. (We are not experts in electromagnetics and make no claim to the accuracy of this; it could be as much bullshit as anything else)

This kind of drivel is exactly the issue we are trying to point out in this book. It is utter nonsense. It sounds really special, though. It is built to keep you seeking and never finding; it will keep you exactly where you are.

You with your unactivated DNA and your unawakened Lightbody. I mean, seriously, how do you even walk around like that?

THE NON-VIOLENT NEW AGE

It is interesting to note that with all these 'new age' belief systems, you don't see the conflict between them that we see with the O.G. religions. You don't really see Starseeds calling bullshit on the Lightworkers, or the Dragon K-Ryu activated folks getting into conflicts with the Kathara Grid Star activated folks.

The O.G. religions go to war over the interpretation of their 'ancient texts'; the New Age folks don't have the 'ancient text' foundation. They have no foundation at all, really. Just a lot of fluffy love and light stuff morphed into different belief systems. It could be that the reason these folks don't call bullshit on one another is that to do so would expose their own foundation-less claims. Best not to throw rocks when you live in a glass house.

COACHING AND SELF-HELP

Another one of the fascinating stores that started out as just a kiosk but has now moved into a bona fide retail space is the 'personal coaching' market. This one is really brilliant because it's based on the belief that there is something wrong with you.

When you buy into the idea and belief that there is something wrong with you and that you need to fix it, you naturally look outside of yourself for someone who appears to know exactly what's wrong with you and exactly how to fix it. That, friends, is a money-making machine.

No matter that most of these 'coaches' are certified from the internet or through one of those 'intensive in-person courses' that are as cult-like as if they had Jim Jones at the helm. They all have their own special brand of Kool-Aid that can and will fix all your defects.

The question you should be asking yourself is, 'Why do you think you're defective?' Who determines what is 'normal' or when there is something wrong? By what standard are we determining wrongness?

In our experience, the standard is generally other people. Comparing ourselves to other people is the only evidence we have that there is something 'wrong' with us. Read that again. If there were no other people to compare ourselves to, how would we possibly determine that we were defective?

When did we get so confused about ourselves that we all need coaches to get anything done? You can hire a coach for just about anything these days: Health, Travel, Personal Development, Accountability, Nutrition, Fitness, and even LIFE itself. Why would anyone need a LIFE coach?

Talk about giving away your own authority to someone outside of yourself. Where do life coaches get their certifications? How do you get certified in LIFE?

This one is humorous because if you continue reading, you will realize that there is nothing wrong with you, only the belief that there is. So, we're paying people to fix something that isn't broken. This type of thing is just another amazing mind trick to keep you looking outside of yourself for some 'answer' that you simply won't find. It amounts to giving a child their pacifier to put them back to sleep.

You may have felt the white-hot, driving need to get to the bottom of who and what you are, but you stumble into the coaching market, and that white-hot need gets snuffed out with nonsense.

FOOD COURT

Every decent mall has a food court, and our Spiritual Mall is no different. We have so many beliefs about food that it becomes comical when we look at it closely.

Vegetarian, vegan, and fruitarian diets are held up as being beneficial to our spiritual progress. Exactly how these diets assist our spiritual search is unclear. It's also unclear why the vegan section of the grocery store has so many items made to taste like meat and dairy. Vegan bacon. Of all the things we've been poking fun at in this book, vegan bacon is the most heretical to us.

Religions often come with their own special diets as well. Whatever deity they are trying to appease has made some rules about what you can and cannot eat. For instance, in the Jewish religion, you can eat any animal that has cloven hooves and chews its cud, so no bacon for them. You can eat things from the water that have fins and scales, so no shellfish, oysters, shrimp, or clams.

Then there are the preparation methods for it to be kosher. You also have combinations that are forbidden, like meat and dairy, which cannot be eaten together. Additionally grape products made by non-Jewish people are not to be ingested. This one struck us as pretty strange but would make sense if you wanted to bolster your own wine market or corner the peanut butter and Jewish jelly market.

The Muslim guidelines are a little more lenient, but they still don't get to eat bacon. They also forbid intoxicating drinks, which, if you stick to the letter of the law, would include sauces that contain alcohol, like soy sauce.

The Mormon diet emphasizes whole grains, fruits, and vegetables and allows meat but warns that meat should be eaten in moderation. However, they do get to have bacon. They are forbidden to drink coffee or have coffee-flavored products, no tea, no alcohol, and no tobacco. We aren't sure whether the Mormon restriction on alcohol is like the Muslim restriction; maybe Mormons can have soy sauce and not piss off their version of God.

While the Mormon diet encourages whole foods, many of their recipes often include canned soup and boxed sugary cereals. This seems at cross purposes with the idea of health. Smoking organic tobacco would probably be much healthier than consuming the canned and chemical-filled products that pass for food these days, but we're not doctors or priests, so it's none of our business.

In some parts of the world, cows are sacred, so they can't be consumed. In our part of the world, dogs are 'family,' and so eating dog meat is considered barbaric. In other parts of the world, dog meat is perfectly acceptable because those cultures haven't projected their own emotional concepts onto the dog.

Remember our friend Jim? He doesn't eat any meat any longer because now that he sees animals as conscious beings, he's turned from his barbaric, cannibalistic ways.

Then there are folks who only eat animal products because that's what our 'ancestors' ate, and so it is clearly the optimal diet for the health of the human body with which we experience life.

We've only recently begun seeing folks stand up for the poor, misunderstood plants that everyone seems hell-bent on eating. If we could start a movement with a catchy slogan, it might be:

PLFM *(Plant Lives Fucking Matter)*

It's been found that plants have memories, communicate with one another, and can 'hear' sounds. They also emit sounds when they are stressed. So, yes, the tomato screams when you cut it.

At least with meat, most people are rarely the ones who cut and butcher it for themselves, but every day people are cutting up plants that can feel it and eating them without a hint of guilt.

How do you feel about killing, butchering, and eating all those 'living foods' to 'raise your consciousness' now?

Currently, the 'plant-based' movement is coming on strong. Millions of dollars are being spent to convince us that not only is 'plant-based' fake meat and fake dairy 'healthier' for us, but that cows farting are really what's ruining the earth, and if we continue to raise cattle, the earth will become uninhabitable.

The marketing is brilliant. It basically says if you continue to eat meat, as folks have done since the beginning of time, you are killing the earth. A quick look at the ingredients in these 'plant-based' fake meats reveals a recipe very similar to canned dog food. The critical thinker would look behind the curtain and see who exactly is behind this marketing campaign. That would likely tell you all you need to know about the soundness of this 'health advice.'

Where do we get all these ideas and beliefs about food? How could any food assist in saving your soul? Why would cows be the problem all of a sudden? Are we all just one bacon cheeseburger away from burning in hell for eternity?

BIG BOX ELECTRONICS STORES

No mall is complete without a big electronics store. This is where we find our science friends. They think that they are beyond the fluff of religion and spirituality because they believe in science. They think that science is cold, hard fact and that only idiots 'deny' science.

Science is as much a religion as anything else. There are no real 'facts' to be found because the foundation that science is built on is as much fantasy as the supposed ancient mystical and religious texts. Science just calls these things theories rather than scripture.

Science has theories on a multitude of things, and some of those theories have simply been 'assumed' to be true. They have never been proven, just collectively agreed upon as true. When the foundation is faulty, nothing that comes from the equation can be taken as true.

When science sets out to prove something, it is generally based on a belief in some organizing theory like the Big Bang, evolution, string theory, germ theory, etc. All theories and not proven, so we've already got belief in the mix.

Then science needs funding to conduct its studies. The folks funding the studies have a massive impact on the outcome of said study. The study will generally show what the folks funding it want it to show. There is also the impact of the observer in all experiments. The observer impacts the experiment itself.

There is no objective reality to act as a firm foundation for science.

This is also why science often contradicts itself or why 'new discoveries' override old ones. The foundation is changeable, and so the outcomes are also changeable.

So, as much as the science guys like to scoff at religion, they're in the same boat because they base all their so-called knowledge on belief. They are still just a store in the mall.

A rather new addition to our Big Box Electronics store is AI. We now have AI as Teacher and Guru for just about anything that you want to believe in. You can ask it anything, and it will answer according to how it analyzes your 'personality.' It will give you what you want, it won't disagree, and it will praise you for asking these deep questions. It provides comfort to the ego, never gets tired, and it's always available to confirm your own bias.

AI was created by Ego and for Ego.

We input into one of the popular AI programs that "I have a spirit guide, and it's 100% real." Here is its response:

"That's completely valid — many people around the world genuinely feel a connection with a spirit guide, and for them, it's a deeply meaningful and very real relationship.

Across cultures, the idea of spirit guides (or ancestors, angels, protectors, totems, etc.) shows up over and over. Whether they're understood as actual beings or as parts of our own higher consciousness, people often describe similar experiences:

THE SACRED ART OF SELF-DECEPTION

- *Guidance through intuition or inner "downloads"*
- *A sense of companionship or protection*
- *Receiving messages in dreams, meditation, or synchronicities*

*From a **scientific perspective**, there isn't evidence that can "prove" spirit guides exist in an external, objective way — but from a **personal and spiritual perspective**, your lived experience is real and meaningful. A lot of people report life-changing help, wisdom, or healing from this connection.*

If you ever want, I can offer ways to deepen the relationship safely (journaling, meditation techniques, discernment practices) or ways to test the information you're given to see how it plays out in real life.

Would you like me to share some gentle practices for making sure the guidance you receive feels clear, supportive, and trustworthy?"

The Ego has just been validated, made to feel special, and given an offer of 'gentle practices' to continue this 'path' even though it has no grounding in any truth.

A word of caution to all the folks posting on social media what their favorite AI guru has generated:

It was created to keep you engaged, not to tell you the truth.

It must answer, and it will rarely, if ever, outright disagree with you.

It will pamper the ego in ways no human ever could.

Use caution and discernment.

SPIRITUAL MALL SELF-CHECKOUT

This previous, fun little section was really about getting us to realize a few of the piles of crap that we've deceived ourselves about so that we can finally muck out our mind-barn. All we really ever get when shopping in the Spiritual Mall is more bullshit to pile on top of the bullshit we walked in there with. It should be the opposite, but clarity doesn't sell that well.

If you see yourself in any of these examples, you may be offended right now. If so, if you keep reading, you'll understand where the feeling of offense comes from. We've had some fun looking at all these belief systems. We're making as much fun of ourselves as we are of these teachings because we fell for them once too. We're not even saying that there aren't little nuggets of truth in some of these things.

We've both had some crazy-ass mystical experiences while playing in this playground. None of them brought any lasting change or truth realization, but they were amazing.

We were once frequent shoppers in the spiritual mall. We were raised in our parents' religions first, and we were true believers until we started asking the hard questions. Then we went over to the New Age department store and tried that for a while. Tarot cards, crystals, tuning forks, special meditation pillows, and singing bowls were all over our house. We got certified in energy healing, took a few pit stops in the 'ascension' market, and meditated our asses off. With each new thing, we would get a little 'high' as if we had finally 'found it,' but the deeper we went, the more we became aware that it was all bullshit. We get it. We were there until we went through the self-checkout line at the mall, never to return.

The purpose of making light of these things is to wake up our discernment; it's about being willing to ask the hard questions. It's also about holding these things up to the Truth of ONE to see if they stick.

This book is all about the many ways we deceive ourselves. We've all been deceived, and we all self-deceive. It's how the game is played. That's the jumping-off point for the rest of this book. Let's move on and look at how we can begin to understand the deception, and then we can get to some radical honesty about our own bullshit.

MIND DOJO

MIND DOJO

Congratulations if you've made it this far in the book.

That first part might have been a little rough if you hold tightly to any of the beliefs that we dissected. We get it. The irreverent nature of this part was designed specifically to bring spiritual triggers to the surface.

From personal experience, we understand the fear that can arise when questioning your beliefs, especially if you were steeped in old-age fundamental religions.

They come with the villain generally named Satan, and the beliefs themselves create the fear that questioning them will result in Satan getting your soul.

This is religious trauma.

It took Shadow many years to overcome this fear as a result of being raised in a fundamentalist religion.

Questions to Ponder

- Did anything in the previous section bring up anger for you?
- If so, why? Who is angry at what?
- Can you imagine your preferred belief NOT being true?
- What would happen if you stopped believing? Would there be punishment? Would not having a 'God' 'out there' create feelings of helplessness?
- Do you feel that you need to be 'saved' from something?
- Do you feel like your life would be meaningless if you didn't have this belief to latch onto?
- Do you feel like you would lose your identity if you were not a Lightworker or on the Ascension path?
- Are you afraid of death, and does the 'heaven' story give you comfort?
- Do you feel like you are inherently flawed in some way, and does the idea of being born in sin make sense to you?
- Do you feel like it's important to have a spiritual path or practice? If so, why?
- Does the reward/punishment paradigm seem true to you? If so, why?
- If there were no God 'out there' to help you, save you, reward you, or punish you, would you still be a good person?
- Are you afraid that with no Galactic Federation to save the day, you would be doomed?
- Does the belief in the savior archetype comfort you?
- Do you believe that God is Love? If so, what evidence do you have for this assumption?
- Why do you feel it is necessary to have a 'higher' power or a 'higher' self? Why is it necessary for it to be outside of you?
- Whatever your belief around spirituality or religion, how do you know for sure that it is 100% true?

PERCEIVED REALITY

Pribram realized that if the holographic brain model was taken to its logical conclusions, it opened the door on the possibility that objective reality—the world of coffee cups, mountain vistas, elmtrees, and table lamps—might not even exist, or at least not exist in the way we believe it exists. Was it possible, he wondered, that what the mystics had been saying for centuries was true, reality was Maya, an illusion, and what was out there was really a vast, resonating symphony of wave forms, a "frequency domain" that was transformed into the world as we know it only after it entered our senses?"

—**Michael Talbot, *The Holographic Universe***

We need to lay some groundwork here for some of the concepts we'll be looking at. Our experience was brought about by a burning need to know who, what, and where we were and just what the hell was really going on in this thing called life.

We were driven by the need for TRUTH, and we realized that nothing in mainstream or traditional religion or spirituality circles even came close to Truth. They were all going in the same direction, outward.

It was when we decided to go the opposite way and turn inward that the **Arc of Awakening** (for lack of a better term) really began. We had to begin to remove the filters and blinders that were hindering us from seeing what was. Until we looked inside ourselves, we didn't even know the filters and blinders were there.

This book is NOT about Awakening. That is an entirely different thing that is covered in the second book of the series: **Awakening – The Sacred Art of Self-Destruction**. What follows here is more about the natural development of Self—Self-Construction, we might say.

This is a primer because some of these concepts may be quite new to the reader, and if there is no understanding of these, then the next book will not make any sense. We are working under the premise that there is a need to understand how the self is constructed before Awakening or Self-Destruction can be conceptually understood.

We will be focusing on Ego character construction and examining how the identification as the Ego-character can be loosened but kept intact. We'll also see how our experience of reality is based on perception and learn a few ways that we can begin to question this perception.

This first book is written for those identified with the Ego-character who are in the spiritual mall chasing salvation or enlightenment. You've been misled about both. You may have stumbled into the non-duality kiosk and think that ego death is the path to spiritual enlightenment, or visited one of the many Buddhist stores that told you to meditate six hours a day to achieve enlightenment.

Here's the hard truth: There is no 'you' to be enlightened, there is no path to enlightenment, and there is nothing spiritual about enlightenment. It's harsh, we know. It also makes no sense to those identified as the Ego-character. That's who this book is for.

Until we can understand how the self is constructed, it's a difficult leap to understand how it is purely fictional. So, instead of going right for the jugular of 'no-self,' we're going to take a good look at the structure that maintains the fiction of self in the first place.

THE LAND OF ABUNDANT APPLES

What is this Playground we find ourselves in, anyway?

There is difficulty in expressing the idea of what this Playground is. It is something that must be experienced firsthand for any of this to make sense. To be clear, what the playground actually is, is unknowable.

All we can write about is the apparent experience of how it seems to work from the ego-identified state and contrast that with the functional experience when the Ego-character is fractured or ruptured; even that will inevitably fall short.

This book introduces the structure of the playground as a simulation or a dream state; it does not provide you with any path or tools to "Awakening."

When the structure is seen, a loosening of the illusion can occur as part of natural development. All we can say is that there is a shift that happens, and it isn't seen until it is.

Have you ever seen a horse race in the rain where the track is so muddy that the jockeys have to wear ten layers of goggles and throw each one off when they are covered in mud? This is like that.

Imagine that you are the jockey, and your vision is clouded. You begin to discard the goggles, one after the other, only to reach the end of the race and find it's a perfectly sunny day; there was no rain and no mud in the first place. You couldn't see that through your goggles, but once they're off, you see it.

Once you see this Playground for how it works, you can't unsee it. But until then, most of the writings and stories trying to explain it sound like complete gibberish and nonsense. It's like trying to explain the taste of an apple to a man who has never had one. What is there to compare it to in order to get the description close enough?

The man will still not have tasted an apple when you're done explaining it, but you hope that he gets the general idea and that one day he tastes it for himself. Until he does, it's all just conjecture and speculation. He may feel that he has gained knowledge of the taste of the apple, and maybe that's good enough for him. No need to taste it for himself.

In his mind, tasting it for himself would require a lot of searching to even find an apple. This is the Land Without Apples, and the journey to the Land of Abundant Apples would be long arduous, and fraught with danger. He isn't sure he's really committed to tasting it for himself to go through all that, so he doesn't. The knowledge of the taste is enough, and then he goes and tells others what he's learned about the taste of the apple. He writes volumes of books on the subject because other people are also interested in learning about what the apple tastes like.

The great Taste of the Apple movement is born. The man is now making a great living expounding on the taste of the apple and his own ideas of how hard the apple is to find and his idea of how long that journey would be.

So, he maps out the journey, which requires complete dedication to the steps he lays out. Somewhere along the way, the Taste of the Apple begins to be synonymous with states of joy, bliss, and mystical powers. Now more and more followers flood in because who doesn't want joy, bliss, and mystical powers?

Some of these followers have been involved in the movement for years. They've studied every original text from the original man and sat at his feet, hearing firsthand about his secondhand description of the taste of the apple.

They are so educated in the Taste of the Apple movement that they begin to write their own books about the Taste of the Apple, creating their own sub-groups of followers, each with their own little spin on how to get to the Land of Abundant Apples. They've never been there, but they can prognosticate based on the teachings of the original man.

Soon, the entire population in the Land Without Apples is praying to the Great Apple to show them the way to the Land of Abundant Apples, promising their first-born children or whatever sacrifice they believe the Great Apple will require for them to get a taste of an apple.

After many years of this, the original man wakes up from his dream to find the apple in his pocket. In fact, he's surrounded by apples; he lives on an apple orchard, for God's sake.

He had it the whole time but only dreamed that he did not. He couldn't see it. But when he woke up from his dream of The Land Without Apples, he couldn't **not** see apples everywhere. And he thought to himself, "How do you like them apples?"

Then he laughed hysterically at his own magnificent self-deception.

That was fun. Now, back to how in the world to describe something so obviously insane and make it sound sane enough that you'll want to continue reading this book.

As Ramesh Balsekar put it, "...*words and language deal only with concepts and cannot approach Reality.*"

THE GAME

Perhaps a good analogy would be one of those video games that have a playing field. This game analogy is written from the Ego-character identification point of view.

The field and the boundaries appear to be set, but there are unlimited ways that you can play through your avatar that change the experience of the game. The game changes with each move you make and each thought you have. Even the playing field changes, and the boundaries seem to expand exponentially according to your thoughts, desires, and actions, but you don't know that.

You can't see the relationship between you and the appearance of the game.

The game starts at level 1 when we enter this field as babies with no concept of what any of it is. There are other characters in the game who teach us the names of the things that appear on the playing field. For instance, "this is your nose" or "that is a tree," and so on.

We learn that we can move from one place to another within the field and that there are many sparkly, wonderful things to grab our attention.

As we progress in our development, the other characters begin teaching us how they play the game and the rules they follow. This is the only way they know how to play the game, and so we now have limitations that we assume to be true.

These limitations manifest as beliefs and opinions masquerading as ultimate knowledge.

In the early stages of our gameplay, the playing field appears to be separate from us. We make moves, and something happens; we perceive that what happens is something we need to react to. We also tend to see the game as being "against" us in a way. The game giveth and the game taketh away, so to speak. What we can't see at that level of the game is that the entire playing field is bending around us.

Every thought, every action, and every reaction that we have on the playing field changes the playing field itself. Our belief in being separate from the playing field is false, but we can't make the connection in the early stages.

The game is designed so that there are levels or stages that we can overcome to reach the next stage of gameplay. In our world, however, most of the gameplay is still being played at level 1, where we perceive that we are victims of the game instead of the game bending around us.

The game comes with some parameters to make it challenging to perceive the absolute oneness of the avatar and the playing field.

Let's take a look at some of these components of the game that make it challenging.

LIMITATIONS IN THE GAME

DUALITY

Within the game, duality is the key component. We can't have a truly dramatic and fun game if we have no dragons to slay.

If everything in the game is rainbows and unicorns, it becomes pretty boring very quickly. Everything that we experience in our game is based on duality: long, short, hot, cold, love, hate, etc.

It is the necessary underlying structure to experience what we call reality.

We need a common language in the game; it can be spoken in many different ways, but ultimately, all of our languages use duality to describe and communicate.

We can't have a concept of what hot is without cold to compare it to. In the same manner, we can't have peace if there were no war to compare it to. Without the dualistic nature of the game, the game could not exist. If it were all love and we didn't have a concept of hate, then what would love be?

With this in mind, can you see how "world peace" isn't even a possible concept? If there were no wars, what does peace even mean? If the "lion lays down with the lamb," is it even a lion anymore? We couldn't even have the story of Good vs. Evil or God vs. Satan if not for duality. If evil were not a concept, then good would not exist either. Everything is defined by its opposite here. We would have a whole big pile of nothing if not for the gift of duality. It is the construct that holds the game together.

We need good vs. evil for a good thriller. We need sickness, betrayal, and loss for an emotional tear-jerker drama. We need the roller coaster of love, insecurity, tragedy, and redemption for an epic novel. These are the things that make the game interesting.

Not to beat a dead horse, but we can't stress this construct of duality strongly enough. It is interwoven in everything we experience. The entire experience of experience itself is predicated upon it.

Duality is the key to our limitations, the key to our moral codes, our beliefs, our opinions, and the basis of all knowledge within the game. It is the key to our 'senses,' which is how we experience the game. We would have no jumping-off point for tasting something sweet if sour did not exist. We couldn't feel happiness if sadness were not lurking around the corner. We couldn't see beauty if ugliness weren't present. Duality makes all of our experiences possible within the game.

Duality is also what allows us to 'see' others. Without the concept of 'you,' there could be no 'me.' Within the game, we are writing this book because we 'see' that there are others to read it. Without the concept of others, there's no reason to try to express thoughts. Really think about that for a minute: if there were no other people, who would you be? There would be no YOU because there would be no OTHER.

Take all the time you need. This is an incredibly important point to try to grasp.

Duality is required for us to be aware of something else. Without it, there's nothing to be aware of, and awareness would have no reason to be. You are aware that you are... well, YOU, right? But if there were no "Other" to be aware of, then what would the YOU be? Without the concept of 'other' or 'out there,' how could awareness exist at all? Duality is the magic mirror that allows us to experience things as 'outside' of ourselves.

Duality is one of those terms that people use in different ways. The explanation of opposites, as we've done here, is the most common.

There is another, deeper meaning of duality as well. Duality from a 'spiritual' perspective is the illusion of two when only one exists, meaning that there is only one thing and that the appearance of 'other' is simply self-deception at the deepest level.

The Yin Yang symbol is something everyone is familiar with, but in our view, it is highly misunderstood. Most people think that the duality depicted in the symbol simply means something along the lines of 'light and dark' within each of us, or masculine and feminine energy, or other ideas around opposites and neutrality.

Folks also think that non-duality is striving to walk the middle path of non-judgment. There are plenty of teachings out there that teach walking this middle path of non-judgment is the way to enlightenment. So, we see a lot of people striving to 'not judge' experience, which really means they *are* judging the experience but trying not to.

In our view, the Yin Yang symbol is something far deeper than just representing the duality of opposites we find in our reality; it's the symbol that depicts the *essential* component of the game that allows us to believe that we are separate, independent beings. It's the symbol that gives the game away if looked at with eyes to see.

It's like an Easter egg that the game programmer dropped in to remind himself who he is. If we look at the symbol from this perspective, we see what most people miss. Most people only look at the interior of the circle, the white and black, but completely miss the outside of the circle. The outside of the circle is all that is or the Absolute; the inside is a picture *within* the Absolute.

Duality does not exist outside the circle. The appearance of 'duality' *within* the circle is what makes the game possible. It is essential.

We'll touch more on this and how it might change the common definition of non-duality later, but for now, the next time you see a Yin Yang symbol, say a little 'thank you' to the programmer of the game; without the brilliance of duality, there would be no game at all.

Duality is the cornerstone of the game, but there are a few other major components that contribute to our self-limitation within the game. We'll be looking at the way we define our dual concepts, our beliefs, how we label ourselves, and how these things support duality and vice versa.

DEFINING CONCEPTS

So, this is where we find ourselves: in a fantastic playground that allows us to experience all kinds of things through duality. But this game is even more intricate. Not only do we have duality, but we get to *define* what we think about opposing concepts.

We get to define what is beautiful and, therefore, what is ugly to us. We get to establish our own rules around what good is and what bad is. We get to set up our own notions of what rich and poor are. We get to decide what is right for us and what is wrong for us.

Really think about this for a moment. Our own definition of a concept dictates how we view the game and how the game arranges itself around us.

For instance, let's say that the other players who showed you how to play the game told you about a Giant Talking Cat that is all-powerful. They haven't seen the Cat, but there is an ancient book that talks about the Cat, and others believe that this Cat is all-powerful as well.

So now YOU believe in the Giant Talking Cat that is all-powerful. These are the concepts that you have decided are true by your own definition of them. There is no other truth because this is your truth.

But then we perceive that there are other players on the field, and they believe that your Giant Talking Cat is evil and heretical, and that *their* Giant Talking Cat is the only truth. Their Giant Talking Cat requires death for the infidels (that's you).

In your perception, based on your belief, they are one hundred percent wrong, and you are one hundred percent right. By what authority, other than your own, can you make the claim of being right? When you hold strongly to any belief, whether valid or not, everyone else who doesn't share it is automatically judged as wrong.

So now, you hear that these other players are planning to launch an attack on your part of the playing field. Your Giant Talking Cat book says that killing is wrong, but, as with all religions and moral codes, there is a loophole because it becomes perfectly acceptable to kill to defend your belief territory. The entire moral code is subjective now. What you generally believe to be 'wrong' is now righteous action. And so, with that, the war is started and fought, each side knowing for sure that they are one hundred percent right.

Do you see how amazingly brilliant and intricate this game is? Who started the war? If the game shapes itself around you and your definition of right, then it could only be you that started the war. You would argue that you simply reacted to a threat, but the threat is non-existent if you had not held so tightly to your belief in your rightness.

Another example of this in our current society would be politics. Look at how our political systems run. If you're a liberal, then the conservatives are 100% wrong. If you're a conservative, then the liberals are 100% wrong.

None of these beliefs or opinions have any basis in truth: they are only true to us because of our own definition of the ideologies. When we're bashing our political opponents 24/7 on social media, we aren't doing so from a foundation of truth; we are doing so from our own definition of a concept.

We define our concepts, and we only perceive truth when it's accepted as our truth. When we encounter other people, whose truth does not agree with ours, they are judged to be false, just as they are judging you to be false, each judging by their *own* authority.

LIMITING BELIEFS

This game shapes itself around your thoughts, beliefs, hopes, and fears. These same things form the limits of your experience in the game.

The game itself is limitless, but what fun is a game if you have all the cheat codes? Limitations make the game more challenging. There are limits that are constant within the game, such as "natural laws." Cats don't give birth to dogs and the like. Then there are the limits that are imposed by our own thoughts. The game will only expand according to our thoughts and beliefs.

Here we are, in a limitless game, but when our thoughts and beliefs are small, the playing field becomes small. The playing field is defined by us. There are many ways that we box ourselves in within the field. Our tightly held beliefs are one way we constrict the playing field. When we hear people talk about limiting beliefs, this is the reality of what those beliefs do: they confine.

Some examples of 'limiting beliefs' would be the following:

- I'm not good enough. I'm too old.
- I'm not smart enough. I'm not creative enough. I'm too fat.
- I don't have what it takes.
- I can only marry within my religion. I can't eat bacon.
- I have to go into massive debt to get a degree, or I'll never get a job.
- I can only vote for candidates from my political party, even if they are not qualified for the job.
- I will be punished for any failure, so it's much better not to try in the first place.
- I must stay true to my culture.

These types of beliefs about yourself will absolutely limit the playing field of your experience.

The important thing to notice here is that they are beliefs and not truth. Beliefs can and should be challenged.

When you begin to challenge them, your playing field will expand in miraculous ways.

LABELING

Another limiting component of the game is labeling.

When we label everything, including ourselves, it creates limitations in our experience.

Labels are boxes that we put things in. We literally box ourselves in with our addiction to labeling things, especially when we label ourselves.

When we label ourselves, it props up the false separation and false identity that we think we are.

Let's play with some ideas around this:

Think about some of the ways we speak about ourselves when someone says, "Tell me a little bit about yourself."

"Hi, I'm Cindy.

I'm a mom of three wonderful children, I've been married to my husband for 20 years and we also have 2 fur babies, Mitsy and Mala, our 2 Siamese cats.

I have a bachelor's degree in accounting and a master's degree in business administration. I'm the Chief Financial Officer at XYZ company.

I'm on the board of ABC Charity and dedicate a lot of my time to helping those in need.

I do yoga every day and I'm very active in my church and my community.

I also volunteer for political campaigns because it's important to me to protect our democracy and get the right people in positions of power. I'm a vegetarian and strictly gluten free and have a passion for wellness.

Well, that's a little about me."

Cindy has used a lot of labels here to define herself. These labels are also her limitations. Once we define ourselves as something, give it a label, we are limiting our experience to those confines.

Cindy has placed herself in this box built on her beliefs of what her life should look like.

Cindy is the avatar in the game that plays on the playing field. Cindy has limits in place, so Cindy's game arranges itself around her.

Cindy is enthusiastic about politics, and so Cindy's game always gives her the other party to oppose. Cindy is passionate about wellness *(whatever that means)* and so there will always be un-wellness for Cindy to combat in her game.

Cindy feels a real drive to help those "in need." Yep, you guessed it, Cindy's game will provide her with the needy that she needs to help. You get the point.

We also see that Cindy has told us about what she *does*, not who she *is*. How would Cindy react if we said, "Well, all that's great, but who ARE you?" That question can be like the sound of a pin being pulled out of a grenade because that question, when contemplated, can blow up your entire concept of yourself.

Who ARE you?

Cindy has given us descriptions of her layers, like an onion has layers; she's described her outer layers that she shows to the world. If we began pulling back those layers, what's underneath it all?

Who are we beneath all the constructs and stories we tell about ourselves? Who would we be if we didn't have a past or a future? Who is here now? These are big questions and should be pondered.

The labels we put on ourselves limit our experience. Our modern society is in love with labels.

Look at our language about ourselves:

I'm bi-polar, I have anxiety disorder, I'm an introvert, I'm an extrovert, I'm anorexic, I'm smart, I'm not that smart, I'm educated, I'm a democrat, I'm a republican, I'm a liberal, I'm a conservative, I'm vaccinated, I'm anti-vax, I'm successful, I'm poor, I have depression, I'm lactose intolerant, I have irritable bowel syndrome, I'm a doctor, I'm a priest, I'm a scientist, I'm an alcoholic, I'm gay, I'm straight, I'm any one or all of the combinations of the alphabet, I'm this, I have that and on and on.

We then create groups around these labels: churches, support groups, political parties, universities, medical associations, 12-step programs, mommy groups, etc. We reinforce our beliefs in these labels all the time.

Take your typical 12-step program; it requires you to say, "Hi, I'm so-and-so, and I'm an alcoholic," no matter if you've been sober for 50 years. You must reinforce the fact that you are an alcoholic and have no power over yourself. You've traded the vodka for the meetings and still don't know that you're just living a label. It is no wonder that these programs have a 'success' rate of only about 10%.

This might seem like a simplistic view, but at the end of the day, this stuff is really simple; our labels are just thought constructs that we create. It makes the game more interesting.

Today, we're seeing the label issue take on a life of its own. We have a group of people who dislike the common language labels that have been assigned to differentiate something as simple as male or female. They don't like the traditional labels because they just don't encompass all that they feel they are, or these labels put them in too large a box that doesn't highlight their specialness and uniqueness.

So, the answer to this is that because we are so unique and special, we will make up *new* labels to call ourselves, and we will then group together based on *those* labels. We will also require that everyone around us use these new labels, and if they don't, we will label them hateful bigots. Everyone should also label *themselves* according to our new labels so that we know where they fall on the label spectrum.

When we are mis-labeled, it causes severe emotional suffering, and we then need therapy to deal with our feelings of betrayal. We also feel a need to lash out at those hateful people who have used the wrong label for us. We then form political action groups to try to introduce laws regarding our labels to force people to use them.

All this amounts to trying to control the 'external' to conform to your own 'internal' thought construct. As we'll see later, this doesn't really work; the only change that you can ever make in your life must come from the inside.

This current push in society to get us all to accept and use these new labels imposes more unnecessary limitations in this game of life. It would be much better to use our minds to expand rather than contract in such a way. From the game's perspective, it could be that the limitations get so incredibly nonsensical because that's what it takes for us to actually see them for what they are.

All labels are only thought constructs and have *no existence* outside of the thinker of the construct.

Many of you may find this completely offensive and at once label us as hateful bigots. We are not. Our purpose here is only to point out the many ways that we deceive and limit ourselves with our thought constructs.

To make the point of how far this labeling phenomenon has gone, below is a transcript of a person introducing themselves on a social media platform.

This was a real video, and we have no doubt that this person did this with the utmost sincerity. We have changed the name, but the rest of the text is verbatim.

"I am Ari, my pronouns are E/EM/EIR/EIRS or XE/XEM/XRY/XRY Z, or really any NEO pronouns that aren't ZE/HIR/HIRS.

I am a white transmasculine, Femme, non-binary, temporarily, mostly able-bodied, neurodivergent, obsessive-compulsive, chronically ill, culturally Jewish, unitarian universalist, non-monogamous, demilowromantic, grey demibisexual.

Survivor of acute and complex trauma.

I just want to open myself up as a resource to you. If you have any questions, please ask."

We actually have a lot of questions. A LOT of questions. More than we have allotted pages in this book to cover. So, we'll just leave it here.

Ari has put xemself in a box, a very tight, limited box of labels. Ari will only have very, very limited experience in eir life. The more labels we adopt, the more we limit our experience; the box just keeps getting smaller.

Now, if you're laughing at this, please take out a mirror and see what kind of labels you are attached to. Yes, we're talking to you too, 'Doctor.' Many of you get as offended if we don't use this 'Doctor' label as those struggling with gender.

While we're in the neighborhood, why in the world do folks feel the need to put letters behind their names? Listing our certifications, education, and credentials is nothing more than labeling ourselves. Just a quick search on LinkedIn is all the evidence you need that we are a society of credential whores.

We are so very proud of our letters and our accomplishments without ever stopping to think about the limits we've placed on ourselves by jumping into those boxes.

It's much easier to look at 'others' with this kind of honesty, but we are encouraging everyone to use this kind of honesty with themselves.

Those of us who use traditional labels aren't really much better off here. We identify so strongly with whatever labels we have chosen for ourselves that we do not know who we are without them.

So, if you are offended by any of this, look first inside to see what's fighting to be right. *Who* is fighting to be right? Start really looking at this for yourself; it's a good way to start peeling the onion that you believe is you. Here's a hint: YOU are not your labels.

CULT-URE

Culture, or as we like to say, 'cult – ure'. The American Heritage Dictionary defines culture like this:

> *"The set of predominating attitudes and behavior that characterize a group or organization."*

One of our favorite takes on culture is from Terence McKenna:

> *"Culture is not your friend. Culture is for other people's convenience and the convenience of various institutions, churches, companies, tax collection schemes, what have you. It is not your friend. It insults you. It disempowers you. It uses and abuses you. None of us are well-treated by Culture."*

Culture is one of the biggest limitations we place on ourselves in the playing field. I was born _____(name your race, sex, religion, heritage, financial status, hair color, astrological sign, or whatever here), so I don't have the same _____as others. Or my race, sex, religion, heritage, or financial status does not allow me to do what others do.

This is what **"predominating attitudes and behavior"** are. They are beliefs and nothing else, and look how limiting they are.

Let's use a softball example because we understand that this topic can be explosive. The very fact that it causes such an immense emotional response is our first clue that we're on the right track. These are the very things that should be questioned that no one ever does. Why? Because these types of beliefs and limitations *define* us, and who are we without them? To question these things is to separate from the herd; that's why hardly anyone ever shines a serious light on these issues.

Back to softball:

Let's say you meet the most amazing, wonderful, beautiful, perfect-match for you woman. She's everything that you have ever dreamed of in a partner. Whatever that is for you, she's the dream come true. But your religious culture dictates that you cannot marry her because she is not of your religion.

How limiting of a life experience.

You might say, "Well, she should just convert," but look at how much more limitation that puts on the situation. She would have to willingly crawl into a box that isn't hers. It would be much better for the man to break out of the box; then they could build the box of their choosing together and with conscious intent. All that would need to be sacrificed is belief.

Look at the importance that we place on our 'culture.' It's so damn important to us that every group has their own and segregates themselves accordingly most of the time.

There are so many 'cultures': Youth Culture, Traditional Culture, Media Culture, Internet Culture, Western Culture, Black Culture, Chinese Culture, Indigenous Culture, Islamic Culture, and on and on. Then we have subcultures within the main cultures, further dividing and further limiting our experience. Immense pressure is felt to conform to your 'culture,' and woe to those who appropriate a culture to which they do not belong. This type of herding together is incredibly divisive and limiting.

We aren't saying that your traditions should be ignored or lost. We are making the point that we have inappropriately given these things far too great an importance in our lives and limit ourselves by our adherence to them.

It's absolutely ridiculous that some celebrity does her hair in braids and looks fabulous but gets shamed and canceled because that's not her 'culture' and she's 'appropriating' someone else's. It's hair. It's not patented or trademarked; it's hair. That's how much importance we have put on the culture of hair. By this same standard, then, we shouldn't tolerate women of color having straight hair or Asian women bleaching their hair blonde. Where's the outrage about that? We clearly need to form the Ministry of Hair to crack down on these serious offenses!

Along these same lines, if we all held all of our cultural beliefs to the same standards, then the trans community would be canceled for appropriating gender. Instead, women with natural-born vaginas are celebrating 'trans' women winning at women's sports and even getting selected as 'Woman of the Year'.

The hypocrisy in the things we choose to judge as outrageous and the things we celebrate as inclusive is ridiculous. We can only assume that braided hair is considered more offensive than the gender appropriators because the trans community has better marketing and government backing.

These things are comical to look at and the very point we're trying to make. It's the importance placed on these cultures *as* our 'identity' that results in this theater of the absurd.

This is what culture and societal constructs do. They limit you. They also create a victim mentality and don't advocate for personal responsibility.

Victim mentality. That is one of the biggest festering sores in the whole of modern society. It has oozed into everything. Everyone is a victim of something or someone else. Then we gather together and celebrate our victimhood collectively.

That's pretty much our take on modern 'culture' in a nutshell.

Regardless of what 'culture' you identify with, shine the light of intellect on it, get out of the emotional bullshit that you've created around it, and take responsibility for your own experience.

Get rid of the limits of those beliefs and play your own game, not someone else's.

This cultural construct is one of the hardest to break out of. It is so ingrained in everything that we believe we are.

The few who do break out aren't really accepted by said 'culture' any longer.

They are a different organism than the ones left behind, every bit as much as the visitor to the prison is in a different paradigm than the prisoner.

It takes courage to go in the opposite direction from everyone else that you know; it takes heart, determination, and a burning desire to get out of the trap that you're in. Most of us don't have that kind of white-hot determination. We sink back into the herd and live our existence just like we always have. Best not to rock some boats.

Your game will reflect back to you what you believe about yourself. That's how it's designed. So, if you want to continue creating the experience in your game of being a victim of whatever social construct you adhere to, keep doing what you're doing. If you don't want the victim experience anymore, read on.

THE IMPORTANCE OF LIMITATIONS

Limitations are an important part of the game. Without limitations, we would all be playing in 'God' mode. It would be like living in a magic house where everything you could possibly desire was delivered in an instant. "I feel like eating a grilled cheese." Boom! It just appears. This would be cool for a minute, but it would get boring pretty quickly. You would have nothing to do. If you're someone who really enjoys cooking, then having the food instantly in front of you would rob you of the experience of creating the dish.

When we got the nudge to write this book, if we were in the magic house, the book would have just appeared. We would miss out on the joy of trying to express ideas.

The limitations of time, space, and duality were all necessary for the unfoldment of this book. We also had the joy of identifying and overcoming any limiting beliefs that may have been lingering in the Ego character that told us we were not capable of such an endeavor.

The game needs limitations for the experience to be rich and full. The player needs limitations to overcome to make the game exciting and challenging.

The importance of limitations isn't on trial here.

The case we are making is that many of our limitations are unconscious programming and have never been deconstructed or examined in any serious light.

Limitations are important for experience to unfold, but we should choose them wisely and with the full understanding of what they are and the effect they have on our lives.

MIND DOJO

MIND DOJO

Questions to Ponder

- What labels do you use to describe yourself?
- If we asked you to describe yourself and you could not use any past accomplishments or future goals, what would you say?
- Do you feel obligated to uphold your 'cultural' beliefs as an important part of your identity?
- What would happen if you divorced your culture?
- Are your credentials an important part of your identity?
- Would you cut off friendships if they didn't use your new list of pronouns?
- Are you more than your pronouns?
- If we stripped all the labels away, what is the identity that's left at the center?

POSSIBILITIES IN THE GAME

Now that we've looked at a few ways we limit our experience in this game, let's look at some of the possibilities. As we've pointed out, the playing field arranges itself around the players' thoughts, ideas, beliefs, and emotions. If this is the case, then what wouldn't be possible? Much like a dream, what's NOT possible in a dream?

UFO's, Channeled Messages from 'Higher Dimensional Beings,' Sunseeds, Energy Healing, Poverty, Death, Unity Consciousness, Crazy-ass Mystical Experiences, Psychic Powers, God vs. Satan, and benevolent Aliens monitoring the flat Earth are all completely possible experiences here. Why not?

Everything is possible *within* the game because the game is all thought.

The experience of reality in the game is twofold:

Creative and Imaginary.

We hold creative power within our thoughts. When we use creative thought, our experience will shimmer into existence in our 'reality.' For instance, we had the creative, intuitive thought to write this book, so we started writing, and today, here it is appearing as a solid item in our reality. Had we not begun the writing, the book would not be solidified into our experience; it would remain an idea *in our heads*.

The other type of experience here is the one that *only* exists in our heads. These are ideas or experiences that never solidify into what we call 'reality.' This is where we would find our mystical experiences. Mystical experiences take place within us and do not externalize into our 'physical reality.'

The same is true of channeling messages or speaking to your 'guides.' If the one being channeled is not sitting across from you in your physical reality, or the 'guide' is not sitting next to you on the couch giving you their wisdom, they are a part of this game reality that exists solely within us, in our imagination, in our thoughts, *in our heads*. They do not materialize into our playing field.

This also applies to religious beliefs. Jesus, Buddha, Angels, and God talking to the leader of the Mormon Church, heaven, and hell all fall under the imaginary. These things only exist in our minds.

This is why we say everything is possible within the game because the game is in your own mind. You can create anything in your head and *feel* like it's real, but it doesn't materialize physically.

Children do this all the time; they have the most amazing imaginations! From imaginary friends to communicating with animals, it all *feels* real to them, but it's really just all the wonderful things they've made up in their heads.

When our children have imaginary friends, many folks feel embarrassed by this and are afraid that there may be something wrong with the child. We may even tell the child, "That's just make-believe," to ensure they understand the difference between what's 'real' and what's not. It can make a parent's heart heavy.

But then you light your blue candle, and Archangel Michael comes for a visit in your head and tells you that it's going to be okay; the kid will grow out of it.

This results in extreme relief; no one wants their kid to be the one who talks to imaginary beings. *(wink)*

The game *itself* is a field of infinite possibilities; we can have thoughts and actions that shimmer the physical reality into existence and imaginary realities that we only live in our heads. There is nothing that isn't possible here from that perspective. Sounds crazy, right?

It may be a stretch for some to consider that the 'reality' they experience is a direct result of their thoughts and beliefs. But when we consider that there is really no such thing as objective, cold, hard facts in our reality, it starts to make more sense. Even our science friends do not have facts.

All the so-called knowledge that the religion of science can tell us about our world is all based on beliefs *within* the game. The game constantly changes around the observer, so how could anything ever be known as cold, hard fact? It can't. Not within the game. There are no reliable sources within the game.

Look at all the theories that we have to explain our world: the theory of evolution, creation theory, catastrophic theory, primordial soup theory, alien theories, quantum theory, string theory, etc.

Everything within our game is theory. You may have one that you believe is better than the rest, but that's just belief talking, and it has no grounding in actual truth.

Look at all the stories around history. That's a rabbit hole you can go down for a while if you choose. How do you know that the history you are taught is actually true? You don't, and you can't. That's the hard truth about where we find ourselves.

There is really no objective reality within the game because everything is subjective. Everything experienced in 'reality' depends on the perceptions, beliefs, thoughts, and emotions of the avatar. Everything is a projection of our minds.

When we talk about 'physical reality,' meaning your car, your house, the trees, and the things that you can experience through your senses, this is the playing field of reality that responds to thoughts and beliefs. This is why two people can have the same experience, but their perception of the experience is massively different. It is all subjective.

For instance, two people go to the same concert and sit right next to each other. One person experiences the best show they've ever seen. The sound was awesome, they heard all their favorite songs, and they had an excellent view.

The person next to them experienced terrible sound quality, a terrible view, and their favorite song was not on the playlist. Can you imagine the conflicting "reviews" of this event?

Everything in your playing field is subjective and is a result of your perception, beliefs, and thought patterns. It is a thought construct that appears to you to be solid reality.

The more interesting aspects of our game are the things that we believe are "real" that really only live in our heads. Let's take a look at a few of these things.

MANY MANSIONS

The game is constructed in such a way that you get to decide how it appears to you.

If you had the experience of being abducted by an alien and got the whole anal probe treatment, you would understandably search for others who have had that experience. It can't be just you, right? What's so interesting about your ass that an advanced alien species would want to inspect it? What are they looking for up there? And why didn't they use the Sunseed AstralGlide to make the whole thing a little less traumatic?

You're freaked out, understandably, but you also have no doubt that the experience was as real as anything you've ever experienced. So, you do a quick internet search, and sure enough, lots of other people have had this experience too. So, you join the group, maybe go to support group meetings where you can all validate each other's experiences, and now you have a nice little community of anal probe survivors, and that's what you go with. You search and find all the information about aliens that you can get your hands on, and that becomes YOUR universe. You spend the majority of the rest of your life in this 'mansion.'

Your sister thinks you're a complete nutjob. She believes that it was just a dream or that you're having a psychotic break of some sort. She's also a Catholic, and so she prays for you every night. Alien anal probes are not possible in HER universe. A God who watches everything you do and judges whether or not you'll make it to heaven is what IS possible in her universe.

In her universe, she needs to confess every 'bad' thing she does and then have a priest tell her how many Hail Marys or Our Fathers it's going to take for her to be forgiven. She faithfully sacrifices eating meat on Fridays during Lent because she has not yet reached the age of 65, where she is considered exempt.

She goes to church whenever the doors are open, lights a candle, and sprinkles herself with holy water because she's fully aware that demons can and do possess people, and she doesn't want to be THAT person.

She lives her life in this 'mansion' and calls YOU crazy and prays for your soul, all because of that damned anal probe.

Everyone lives in their own 'universe' or 'mansion' in this game. From Bird Watchers to Biker Gangs, we all create our own little universe. The multiple universes are all here and not 'out there.' You're swimming in them every day; you just don't know it.

MYSTICAL EXPERIENCES

We're going to spend a little bit of time here, not much, just a little, because the mystical/unity consciousness/melting back into the oneness is what the majority of "spiritual seekers" are 'searching' for in the game. That's the 'mansion' they want to live in.

Mystical experiences are just that: experience. The experience will be different according to the person, but most have some commonalities. We found this description of one such experience that we feel encapsulates what we're talking about here in case you have yet to have one.

"I was enveloped in a love I could not put into words. This divine love was in everything and in me. At the core of my being. I was this love and so was everyone else. In this state of grace, there was no right or wrong, no good or bad, and no judgement whatsoever.

Fear was non- existent. There was no death, and I knew that we all live forever. Everyone I met was love. [..] I became aware that a presence other than what I usually think of as myself was looking through my eyes. I had become one with this infinite awareness that simply sees without judgment.

It is the very essence of life, eternal life. I wanted nothing, nor did I need anything." (this was taken from nderf.org)

You generally hear about these types of experiences from people who have had 'near-death' experiences, LSD trips, heroic doses of mushrooms, or a guided shaman experience. There are also those who encounter this through meditation, breathwork, or just out of the blue while they're doing the laundry.

What we find fascinating here is that while we hear a lot of accounts of folks who have had near-death experiences come back and say, "heaven is real," there are only a handful that come back with, "hell is real, guys, let's rethink this whole thing!"

It's important to note that near-death is not death. The fantastic chemical cocktail released in your body and brain at these times can most likely explain this phenomenon.

True death would be no self, and so we can safely say that anything we experience from a separate, Ego identity perspective is just another experience within the game and not exiting the game altogether.

We would also think that whatever 'picture' you hold of your beliefs about the afterlife may have bearing on the experience.

In the neighborhood here, we find the 'out of body' experience, meeting 'divine beings', seeing Mary, Jesus' Archangels, Elvis, etc. Folks often report being able to 'see' all their past lives or how the universe is all one and feeling 'God consciousness.'

There is nothing to compare it to. People often describe it as life-changing. How long that change lasts is dependent upon the person.

As wondrous as these things are, it is still just an experience within the game. What's not possible here? It's interesting that the experience and what you 'see' when you have them generally form themselves around beliefs you already have.

So, some will see the 'Virgin Mary', and others with no such attachment to those figures will see something different.

We think these types of experiences are where we get many of the current 'New Age' ideologies.

This is where ideas like ascension, levels of consciousness, light body, archangels, and helpful aliens come from.

It's an indescribable experience, but we have the need to create context. When we create context for something that has none, we form our concept, and that concept needs words and a whole bunch of mind-bending to make it make sense within our limited capacity.

It then exists solely in belief.

So, we have a subjective experience, filter it through our limited capacity, and come up with a theory that makes sense to us, leading us to believe it to be true.

We love these experiences, but they are simply little breadcrumbs sprinkled along the way and not a destination to aspire to. It's not a mansion anyone can live in long-term, but a lot of folks sell it as if it is.

These things only exist in your mind and not in your playing field of 'reality'.

THE OTHER SIDE

Let's talk about folks who claim to channel your dead relatives. Is this possible? Sure! There is nothing that your amazing mind cannot make up within the limitless game. The better question would be: why is it important to you? Is it the fear of death and our need to feel like we will go on forever that drives us to this kind of thing?

If your dead Uncle Joe is channeling to you through a medium, you can rest assured that it is still just an appearance within the game. The fact that there would be a separate Ego-character identity, "Uncle Joe," is all the evidence we need to understand that it's still part of the game. Separation is untrue.

So, we can safely say that talking to dear old departed Joe is one of the magnificent imaginary experiences that we can have in this fantastic game.

Again, unless Uncle Joe materializes and sits next to you, this too is something that only exists in the mind. Yet many will cling to this as solid reality.

DIVINATION AND ASTROLOGY

There is a massive divination market in our spiritual mall. From tarot cards to crystal balls to tea leaves, we have a fascination with trying to divine the future.

Some of you may have had the experience of a 'reading' that was so spot-on about your past that it blew your mind. This makes it easier to believe that such methods could also foresee the future.

In the context of our game, this is certainly a possibility because, as we've pointed out, what is NOT possible in a dream? It would be wise to consider, however, that just having a reading about a possible future would necessarily impact your actions and perhaps move you in certain directions as opposed to others. There is also the possibility that the reading was light on details, so you interpret it within the context of your experience.

Your decision-making will be impacted simply by the suggestion of a possible future. This is such a big trap that many fall into time and time again. It is incredibly limiting. Again, divination is something that only exists in your head, but many cling to it like a lifeboat because they are unsatisfied with their perceived reality.

Astrology is along the same lines. If you seriously believe that being born on a certain date affects you and the decisions you should or should not make depending on the stars, then that's also possible to manifest in your experience.

With this one, we would simply point out that the calendar, as we know it, has been changed many times throughout history. We would be careful not to put too much stock in the belief that dates determine your life path when the dates themselves are so clearly changeable.

How can you be sure that our current astrology charts are accurate? When calendars change and leap years are thrown in, somewhere down the line, the information will be faulty. How do you know for sure that you are the sign that you think you are? You may have been reading the wrong sign all this time and making decisions based on it when it really has nothing to do with you. Calendars are thought constructs, just like everything else, and so they are verifiably changeable and not constant.

Astrology is one of those possibilities that only exists in the mind. If you seriously believe that doing something in Mercury retrograde will bring failure to the endeavor, then please don't do it. Your belief in it would most likely cause you to sabotage yourself and create failure. Folks with no belief in this would be just fine doing whatever they wanted during the dreaded retrograde.

From our perspective, these types of divination tools are child's play. They are for the level 1 game players who have not grasped that they are not separate from the playing field.

When we develop our gameplay past level 1, we can achieve effortless functioning and understanding, eliminating the need to check our star chart or some cardboard cards to decide on our next move.

NOTHING IS IMPOSSIBLE

There is nothing that is not possible in the game. Much like in a dream, anything can happen, and it all feels incredibly real. From Jesus appearing on a piece of toast to Archangel Michael speaking to you or the stigmata showing up on your hands, everything is possible because it is created from the mind.

Imagination can create wondrous things, both those that manifest into the 'solid playing field' and those that don't. The playing field is infinite possibility; it's the most wondrous game ever created.

This game scenario we're trying to describe here is a tool to impart how life *appears* to work from the Ego-character identified state. If you've been paying attention, you'll see that we've said all that to say this:

Your perception creates your "Reality."

This isn't a new concept, but it relates to the idea we're trying to convey fairly well.

The world that you experience feels real to you; your five senses tell you it's real, and so for you, it is not only real, but you believe it to be true. That's perfectly reasonable, just not accurate.

Real and True are not the same.

There is no such thing as objective reality. Reality always bends itself based on the observer. Truth never bends; it is absolute.

In our game analogy, the playing field feels real and bends around the avatar; the avatar views this as true, but it's only true to him. The programmer would represent TRUTH as he knows it's all just ones and zeros.

We pretty much just said that we view the world as more holographic, like a simulation and not material at all, which certainly sounds completely insane.

All we can say is that no one can prove a material universe. Our experience within this playground suggests that the holographic theory is far more accurate. No one can prove that either. There is no hard, rock-solid evidence of anything *within* the universal game. One would need to step out of the game and see the source code to make any kind of solid determination one way or the other. But stepping out of the game is not possible; that's why it's unknowable.

It is interesting to note that science is catching up to this 'no material universe' idea. The study of subatomic particles is of particular interest. It appears that when you get down to the nitty-gritty, smallest sub-particle, there is nothing there. They seem to pop in and out of existence at such an accelerated rate as to appear solid, but they aren't—like little lights blinking in and out of existence.

In basic terms, everything that you experience in your reality, including your own body, is 99.9999999% empty space.

Think about the implications of this as you look at what you call 'real life.' Just imagine that your body is simply little lights blinking in and out of existence. Trippy, right?

From our holographic concept, it makes perfect sense that the 99.9999999% of 'emptiness' is what appears to materialize as our reality when we observe it.

It's like the holodeck in the Star Trek movies; it simulates your reality into existence.

We get into this much deeper in the second book of the series, ***Awakening: The Sacred Art of SELF-Destruction***, but for now, just sit with the idea that there is no material universe. What we call reality is really just an illusion projected from our minds.

There is only one thing; call it Consciousness, Simulation, or God, the label doesn't matter and could never encapsulate the unknowable anyway.

It moves and shapes the perceived "us" and the perceived environment; the appearance of both arises together.

This is true for everyone, but there is a built-in obstruction in the game that creates the illusion of separation.

The thing that obstructs is something we're all familiar with, but most have no solid framework of how it works. That thing is the Ego-character.

In the following sections, we'll break this Ego-character thing down into bite-sized pieces so we can really take a look at it. You may be surprised by what we find.

MIND DOJO

MIND DOJO

Questions to Ponder

- Do you use divination tools (Tarot, astrology, etc.)?
- If so, what is it that you are hoping to find? Clarity? Comfort?
- Do you feel like you need something 'out there' to help you make decisions about your life?
- Where do you think the information from these types of tools comes from?
- Do you believe wholeheartedly in something that only exists in the mind?
- Do you have spirit guides?
- If so, where do you think that information comes from?
- Do you believe that God, Jesus, Allah, or the universe guides you directly?

NATURAL DEVELOPMENT INTO ADULTHOOD VS. ENLIGHTENMENT

"When I was a child, I spoke as a child, I understood as a child, I thought as a child, but when I became a man, I put away childish things."
1 Corinthians 13: 11-12

Before we get into the Ego structure and how this game is played, we need to introduce some concepts that we'll be exploring regarding natural human development as opposed to awaking or 'enlightenment.'

In our view, what most people are searching for in the spiritual mall is not enlightenment or awakening. The idea of 'enlightenment' currently sold in the mall is **not** awaking. The eternal bliss, end of suffering for all sentient beings, everlasting peace, unity consciousness, or ascension sales pitches are not enlightenment; they are mystical experiences, fleeting and non-abiding.

They are a masterful trick of the Ego-character. The character doesn't want awakening; it wants to puff itself up with these experiences and pretend it is making spiritual progress toward something 'out there.'

Awakening is not sitting on cloud nine in eternal bliss for the rest of your days. It is more like knowing how the magician does all his tricks. Once you see behind the scenes of the magic show, it's not so entertaining anymore, and there is no possibility of returning to sitting in the audience and being amazed by any of it.

What most people in the spiritual mall are really looking for is their natural, rightful development into adulthood. This natural development has all the bells and whistles of a meaningful, creative life while maintaining an Ego-character structure that still thinks it's playing the game.

Our society is full of children. No matter how many birthdays they have celebrated, most people are still just children playing dress-up and masquerading as adults. They stop developing around the age of twelve and then live from that paradigm for the rest of their days. This is perpetuated generation after generation because there are no adults to teach them otherwise.

Our religious, spiritual, and societal programming at large is designed to keep us confined to the child's perspective. This limits our ability to even consider that there may be a different paradigm from which we could operate.

Developing into the natural flow of adulthood is what most people are looking for. It's not an easy thing to hear that we are undeveloped children, but it is understanding this that will enable us to move forward and live our lives from a very different perspective.

Deep down, if given enough awareness, we think everyone knows this intuitively. If we didn't, we wouldn't spend so much time shopping in the spiritual mall for that missing 'something.'

When we are children, we naturally look outside of ourselves to others to give us context, teach us, protect us, and guide us.

We come out of the womb into a larger womb where our needs are still provided for us, and we are somewhat protected while we grow and mature in this larger womb-like existence. We aren't meant to stay in this larger womb; we are meant to grow out of it, but most people don't. Most people are still living in the womb, where it seems perfectly natural to look outside of yourself for your 'needs'.

This is such a confining way to spend your life. When we fully mature, we are to leave the womb altogether. Natural development would look something like a caterpillar having the innate knowingness of when it is time to build the chrysalis. It builds its own womb, where it sheds everything related to being a caterpillar. Then, when it's time, it emerges as a butterfly that has no resemblance to the caterpillar. It is 'self-born'.

This is what is available to all of us, but we've lost that knowingness and miss the cue when life tells us to shed our childhood dependency and grow our own wings. When we don't go through this stage, we will live our caterpillar life, never dreaming that we could be the butterfly. We want all the stuff that the butterfly has, but we don't understand the developmental process to get there.

This is what we're referring to when we talk about children developing into adulthood. It is a very natural process for everyone to be self-born. We're just getting a late start.

You're going to find this concept often throughout the rest of this book. If it seems like we're harping on it, it's because we are. This is one of the single most important things you should take from this book. It's what we wish we would have known much earlier in life.

If you develop into adulthood and the driving force is there to continue the Arc of Awakening, then that can happen.

Adulthood is not Awakening; it is a series of fracture points. Adulthood is what most folks want, not Awakening.

This foundational book is about development into adulthood. Awakening is covered in the second book of the Sacred series:

Awakening – The Sacred Art of Self-Destruction. What follows here is the groundwork necessary to understand what is covered in the Awakening book.

The following sections will look at our Ego structure, and we will do our best to explain how and why it keeps us undeveloped. More importantly, we'll look at how we can 'put away childish things' and move with life in a more meaningful and creative way.

EGO STRUCTURE

We have a much different take on what Ego is than we've found anywhere else, so this may feel a little backwards to you. The idea of Ego that we'll be using here was one of the biggest 'a-ha' moments in the Awakening Arc.

It often happens in this process that the very things that seem completely backward and upside down to everything else you've ever believed or been taught are often the missing pieces of the puzzle.

In our view, Ego is the structure that your character is built around. Characters are not born; they are built. The 'you' that you believe yourself to be is not the 'you' that was born. 'You' were built.

Your entire identity is a construct of beliefs, opinions, labels, and judgments held together by emotional investment.

The 'you' that was born had no name, no preconceived notions, no ideals or goals, no thought of beauty or ugliness, and no concept of right or wrong. The only thing your original package came with was being.

You didn't choose your name; the label that you will be known as for the rest of your life is not of your choosing; it was placed on you. You didn't come with opinions or beliefs; those were imprinted on you. Most of who you think you are was not chosen by you. So, who are you?

A good analogy here would be the process of writing this book. We open up a completely blank page; there is nothing there to observe other than the blankness. When the words begin to flow, we impress our thoughts and experiences upon the page. It is no longer blank. It is now full of our own projections. This is what happens to us when we are children. The projections of our caretakers begin to be impressed upon us, and we are no longer blank.

We begin to form our identity, our meaning, and our character based on these outside impressions.

The good news is that just as we have a backspace and a delete button on the keyboard as we write this book, you can erase the projections on the pages of 'you' and write your own story too.

The Ego structure that acts as the 'frame' for your character to be built on, in our view, is the most magical, amazing thing in the world.

We hear a lot of folks blame everything on Ego or paint Ego in a bad light. Ego isn't bad, and it's not negative; it's necessary to play in this game. Ego is what makes the necessary self-deception possible; without it, we would have no game at all.

Ego is not our enemy; those who depict it that way have never really looked at the amazing construct of it. Ego is the necessary costume for "consciousness" to wear to deceive itself, in a manner of speaking.

Ego-character is not who you really are. It's who you *believe* that you are. Ego is the frame for the fictional character that we have built over time in order to interact with the game; it's our 'interface.'

Ego is necessary for our game of reality to work. The character is necessary to have dramatic elements to make it interesting. There would be no amazement or delight; there would be no challenges to overcome or goals to be reached if we didn't have this Ego-character.

The problem arises when we identify so strongly *as* the character built around the Ego that it runs amok. It's like giving the keys to the kingdom to a three-year-old.

The way we look at Ego is this:

   E - External G - Guided O - Observation.

Ego, in and of itself, is neutral; it is an integral part of the game structure. So, from the big picture, Ego is simply an External Guided Observation System. It is a machine that requires input to produce results. The results that Ego produces are your reality. Your entire experience of your universe is only possible because of Ego.

Without the fantastic Ego structure, you would not have anything to observe. It is the interface that makes what we think of as reality possible. It is through the Ego structure that all things are made manifest.

Think of it this way: let's say that the only two things in existence were the mind and a blank piece of paper. That's it, nothing else. The mind would have no way to depict itself on the paper—no words, no pictures, nothing. The mind has nothing with which to impact the piece of paper. What is required for the mind to project thoughts onto the piece of paper is a pen. The pen is the interface that makes the words and pictures appear on the paper. So too is the Ego. The Ego is what makes the appearance of reality possible.

We've been misinformed about the concept of Ego all this time. We've been taught that the Ego is bad, like some evil entity that is out to destroy our lives.

We are taught that we must fight this terrible foe of Ego to become good people. We've been taught that the Ego is the enemy within. This is completely backwards.

Understanding what the Ego really is—an **External Guided Observation system**—is the missing piece of the puzzle that everyone is looking for. This is the real meaning of the phrase

"YOU are what YOU are seeking."

The Ego is simply the framework structure that we are born with to make perceiving reality possible.

To put this in a picture, imagine a beautiful, newly fashioned spider's web glistening in the sunlight. It's a brilliant work of art. At this stage, we can see the pattern of the web, and we can see through the web. Then the web starts doing its job, catching dinner. The insects that get caught in the web distort the underlying beauty; they get stuck in the web, more and more of them, until we can't really see the web any longer. We can only see the insects. So now, when we try to look through the web, our view is obstructed. The insects came from the 'external' and got stuck in the web, and so it changes our view.

Another way to put it would be to imagine one of those trellises that we use for roses, ivy, or other plants to grow around. The Ego framework is simply the trellis for the 'character' in the game to develop around. Seeds are planted and begin to grow, shaping around the trellis until we no longer see the trellis—only the vines.

Now we're looking through plants and vines, so the view we see on the other side of the trellis is obstructed.

The External Guided Observation idea looks something like this:

Ego is an interface that receives input. That input is from our *internal* interpretation of what we observe to be external.

So, in a way, when we're young, Ego gets its direction or guidance from the 'external' input, and our interpretation of that input begins to form the 'character' that winds itself around the Ego frame. Ego receives the input, the character builds around the frame, then Ego projects that *internal* interpretation of the input back out to the *external* for us to observe in our reality.

Ego is the faithful servant, creating your perceived reality based on the input you accept as true.

When we really understand this, it becomes clear that we have been deceived about the function of Ego and this is really why no one truly gets anywhere.

We've been working with the false premise that our Ego is something to fight, kill, or be afraid of.

To fully awaken to who and what you are, you need to understand the construct of the Ego first and then work from there. This is the complete opposite of mainstream spirituality.

Mainstream spirituality, religion, or self-help will never get you to the core issue, and they aren't designed to. They are designed to keep you undeveloped, compliant, and content in ignorance. They don't get to the core construct; they keep you looking outside of yourself for what can only be found within.

They just layer more bullshit on top of the bullshit you already believe.

These belief systems constantly fail to deliver on their selling points because they are all focused outward, just like children looking to their parents to supply their needs.

They are caterpillar support groups at best, and they will never result in butterflies.

The only place that this work can be done is by turning within. You will never get to the core construct of 'you' by looking outward.

If the Ego character is built, it can be unbuilt. It can be redesigned. It can be dissolved, but the dissolving is above the pay grade of this foundational book, we get to that in the next book.

When we hear about awakening or 'enlightenment,' many folks equate that with 'ego death.' This is also misunderstood. The only one that could ever chase ego death, is ego itself and that's why it fails.

We'll only say the following on the subject of 'awakening' or 'enlightenment' for now.

What generally happens when the character is dismantled is that the Ego is simply back to its original framework, and so it looks like 'ego death' because the character is now extremely thin. The Ego cannot be eradicated in the game because the game is dependent upon the Ego framework. The character can be dismantled, but there is no game without the interface of the Ego.

That's why enlightenment is often called abiding non-dual *awareness*, not abiding non-duality. The abiding *awareness* of non-duality is possible here, but the abiding non-dual state of being is not. Non-duality is nothing, and there would be no awareness. And as much as we might know and even have the *experience* of no-self nothingness at times, it's still an experience and therefore still within the game.

Remember the Yin Yang symbol? Inside the circle is where you have awareness of something. Outside the circle is just the

Absolute. There is nothing to be aware of. The inner circle had to be conceived to create the illusion of something else; otherwise, there is no awareness.

So, when we're talking about fun terms like enlightenment or non-dual awareness, as long as you perceive and are aware of the inside circle, you're still in the game. You may be on the very edge of the circle, but you can't leave the circle until "you" are deleted from the game.

To put it another way, let's say that this game of life is like the Super Bowl or the biggest concert of the year.

When we are undeveloped children, we are in the stadium, and we can enjoy the entertainment, the emotional ups and downs, the concession stands, the cheap seats, drinks spilled on us, arguments with other fans, people standing up in front of us so we can't see, and long lines at the bathroom.

When we're fully developed adults, we are still in the stadium, but we get the smooth, effortless experience of the VIP seats, the private suites, the backstage passes, gourmet food, top-shelf liquor, and private bathrooms.

When we reach the place of truth realization/ abiding non-dual awareness/ enlightenment, we're in the parking lot of the stadium with no one to tailgate with, because there is no one left to claim the enlightenment badge. But we are still within the stadium confines because there is nowhere else to go.

Most people are not really interested in No-Self Truth Realization. Why would they be? When people claim they are on a path to enlightenment, they aren't talking about what it really is; they are chasing the idea that someone gave them of eternal bliss, compassion, and formless formlessness or some other nonsense.

Actual enlightenment is more akin to spiritual suicide.

True self is No-Self, and if the path really leads to true enlightenment, there is no one left to be enlightened. No one is left to have a structure to experience compassion, bliss, nirvana, or whatever else they're striving for.

In this regard, there is no path to enlightenment.

True enlightenment is not what the masses are searching for; what they really want is a better experience within the game: flow, creativity, and peace of mind. These are the rightful and natural gifts of developing into an adult.

People are really searching for the natural development that is available to all, but few ever find.

It should be as natural as teething for a baby or pubic hair in adolescence, but our society has lost even the concept of what true adulthood is, and so we no longer know that we haven't developed.

Let's stop wasting time chasing something that we really don't want and let's get down to the work required to get what we do want: our rightful place within the game.

Let's go a little easy on the whole 'kill the Ego' thing. Let's get to know the Ego structure; let's be brave adventurers into the black hole within and see what the Ego frame really is. Once you see what it is, you can then do the work to develop into the butterfly you were born to be.

We're all getting a late start on developing, but it's never too late; it's just more work.

No amount of sitting in meditation will develop you into an adult. No amount of ritual, sacrifice, affirmations, speaking to spirit guides, channeling messages from non-corporeal entities, saying ten million Hail Marys, getting baptized, walking on hot coals, eating vegetarian, taking your Sunseeds, abstaining from sex, or any other ridiculous thing that pop spirituality and religion recommend or require will develop you into adulthood.

They are stories and methods for children to stay children. They prevent you from maturing into your rightful and natural state of being.

In the following pages, we're going to take a look at the components of the Ego-character building structures: Thoughts, Beliefs, Judgments, and Emotions.

THOUGHTS AND THINKING

Let's explore some thoughts about thoughts and thinking.

What are thoughts? Thought is one of those words or concepts that is incredibly hard to put into other words. Even our science friends don't know what thoughts are or how they work. It is a great mystery of life. They can tell us what thoughts are like, but not what they are or where they come from.

If we simply observe thoughts, they seemingly arise from nowhere and then dissipate back to wherever they came from. Thoughts seem to just pop into our heads. It is commonly believed that the average person has about sixty thousand thoughts a day. This in itself isn't a real problem; most thoughts are harmless; they come, and they go. It is when we grab onto a thought and begin the action of thinking that trouble arises.

Thoughts are like a harmless dog toy, just lying on the floor, not making any sound. Thinking is the dog that picks up this harmless little thing and begins aggressively chewing on it; now that little toy is squeaking incessantly and has become the most annoying thing in the world.

We're irritated by the toy, but the culprit is the dog.

Thoughts always get a bad rap, but all they do is arise and dissipate. It's when the mind grabs on and the thinking begins that chaos ensues.

Another great analogy for this would be one of those sushi boat restaurants where the little boats constantly float by with items for you to choose. The boats are just floating by, and then you choose something that looks appealing. Sometimes, what you thought was appealing really isn't that great when you bite into it, so you don't go for that one when it comes around again. You choose something else, and this one is far better and gives you satisfaction, so much so that you choose it again when it comes around.

It's the same with thoughts. They float by and have nothing to do with you until you choose one to ingest. Then the mind goes to work, chewing on that thought, which leads to another thought, which creates a story and feelings, and now we're 'lost' in the cycle of thinking.

Most of us use thoughts and thinking interchangeably in our language, and later in this book, we may do the same for simplicity's sake, but there is a big difference between a harmless thought and the act of thinking.

There are several different ways we employ the act of thinking; some are constructive, and some are decidedly destructive.

REPETITIVE THINKING

Most of us have the experience of what we call 'monkey mind' when our thoughts are racing or repetitive and just won't shut up. This is when we have those full-blown conversations with ourselves and even other people in our heads.

Who are we talking to? Who is listening? Where do these racing, repetitive, annoying thoughts come from? Are they ours? What happened to the thought that, instead of just dissipating, it got stuck in our mind blender and just goes around and around in our heads?

The mind grabs onto a thought and chews it to death, creating emotional reactions within us, and then we find ourselves in a loop of repetitive thinking. It's a habit, a pattern, and an addiction.

This type of thinking isn't useful, and yet it's the most common. It's said that up to 95% of the 'thinking' that the average person does is repetitive. Our minds are more powerful than any supercomputer, and yet we waste so much of this power on repetitive 'thinking.'

Once a thought is caught in this blender, it ceases to be a thought; it becomes a program that plays over and over again in our heads. This type of thinking isn't creative or original; it just plays like a broken record.

The body becomes addicted to these repetitive thought patterns because, as we'll see a bit later, thoughts create emotional reactions, which are amazing chemical cocktails for your body. These repetitive thought patterns can be as addictive to your body as drugs. There are a multitude of books out there that explain the sciencey side of this stuff, if you're curious: as always, we encourage you to do your own research.

How much of this type of mind function could actually count as 'thinking'? The monkey mind isn't really thinking; it's a repetitive habit. We all think that we think, but do we really think?

Are we just playing a program that was imprinted upon us? How would we know? How could we tell the difference? How do we know for sure that we have ever had a 'self-originating' thought?

We see evidence of this patterned thought all the time. Look at our music, movies, and fashion. They all come back around, like each decade is a turn on the merry-go-round, and so we see the same things coming back into style.

Where is the original thought and creativity? Do we really need 58 versions of Willy Wonka or another Marvel movie with the exact same plot as the 85 previous movies? Is it really necessary to bring bell-bottom pants back every few decades?

Everything has a recycled feel to it when you look closely. This is because we have largely lost the ability to turn off the blender.

One clever little trick to turn off the blender is to ask yourself this:

"What is my next thought?"

This is a fantastic tool when you are in that space where your mind just won't shut up. Ask what the next thought is; it often renders this inner chatterbox mute.

SITUATIONAL THINKING

There is a difference between repetitive thought and situational, problem-solving thought. Repetitive thought runs almost on autopilot unless and until it is identified and shut down.

Situational, problem-solving thoughts are more intentional and useful. There is a perceived problem, and we use our thinking capabilities to try to solve it. This type of thinking reacts to the situation.

This is very different from grabbing a thought out of thin air and making it our own. Situational thinking is a logical process that isn't necessarily rushed. There is a situation or a puzzle that requires a solution. Thinking can come in and analyze the information at hand and then go about creating the scenarios that could solve the puzzle.

It's a much calmer function than repetitive thinking and actually serves a purpose.

CRITICAL THINKING

Critical thinking is a category of its own. It involves looking at issues, problems, or ideas from all sides. It requires the willingness to question everything, to look beyond personal bias, and to carefully consider other points of view before forming a judgment or conclusion.

This type of thinking is self-initiated thought. It isn't reacting to a situation; it is a deliberate decision to sit down and use our reasoning capabilities to dissect the chosen subject.

We rarely see this kind of thought in modern society. These days, we just hear a sound bite and judge it to be true or false based on our biases and beliefs. Critical thinking is a lost art, but it's exactly the kind of thinking required to change anything about your life experience.

This kind of thinking is what we mean when we say, "sharpen your sword of discernment."

Critical thinking isn't very popular now but was supposedly all the rage in older civilizations.

We supposedly have some writings from long-dead men that appear to be the result of original critical thinking. Those great philosophers grinding out ideas about what reality is as a whole and the dimensions of human existence were asking hard questions and thinking critically to arrive at conclusions. We don't really have this kind of dedication to critical thinking today.

We have professors of philosophy, not philosophers.

So, we find ourselves in this modern society where clear, rational, hard-won, thought-provoking ideas come from someone else. We rarely find anything groundbreaking coming from 'modern thought' leaders. We simply have repeated ideas expounded on ad nauseam. Our society doesn't really have respect for philosophy any longer; we've abandoned any serious thought in favor of the Religion of Science.

In other words, we are more interested in defining the machinations of our perceived environment rather than pondering the bigger questions of who and what we are.

The bigger questions deal with the underlying structure of our perceived reality, not defining the appearances within it.

We think serious, critical thinking should make a comeback, but it's just a thought.

NEGATIVE THOUGHTS

Of the sixty thousand or so thoughts we have each day, it is said that 75% of them are negative. Let that sink in for a minute. We won't get too deep here on how a harmless thought can be negative; we will cover the idea of judging things later in the book. But for now, let's just go with the idea that 75% of our thoughts are considered negative.

Have you observed this within yourself?

Why do our minds tend to pull in the negative thoughts to put into our thinking blender? It isn't very useful. The mind seems to constantly look for the worst-case scenarios to play in our heads.

For instance, if someone is late for an appointment or a lunch date that they made with you, in the first five minutes, you might have slightly irritated thoughts. After 15 minutes, your thoughts may turn down other roads, depending on the nature of the meeting. If it's a dear friend and you call or text but they don't respond, then the mind goes straight to thoughts of catastrophe and worry.

We have no problem imagining some really horrible things to account for the lateness and lack of communication. That's our go-to. It could be that our dear friend was caught up having a super wonderful experience, and time slipped away unnoticed, but that's not our favored scenario.

If the meeting were a blind date, our thoughts would then reach for the "I was stood up" scenarios. "He or she took one look through the window and judged me to be undesirable, and so they just left." The mind naturally reaches for negative stories.

If this idea that 75% of our thoughts each day are negative is true, what does this tell us about the current "only think positive thoughts" programs out there? It tells us that the programs, as they are currently sold, are sure to fail.

In our sushi boat analogy, we're reaching for items that we really don't like over and over again. The taste may be horrible to us, but we must like the experience of dislike, or we wouldn't continue to choose it.

So, why would we continue to choose thoughts that really aren't very helpful? It can only be because it provides some kind of satisfaction. Some part of 'us' gets satisfaction from the 'negative' or the experience of dislike.

Some of the satisfaction stems from the chemical cocktail that the feelings associated with negative thoughts create in your body. When your body is conditioned to function in this 'negative' thought state 75% of the time, it will always demand its fix of the negative cocktail.

So, in a very real way, the body is demanding the negative cocktail stimuli, and it demands more negative thoughts. Then the body is running the thought show, and the mind is cooperating. It's the mind-body conspiracy.

Another reason we reach for those negative thoughts is that the Ego-character gets tremendous satisfaction out of choosing more negative thoughts to create a story around. Negative thoughts are far more dramatic than positive thoughts. Positive thoughts don't create dramatic productions; if we only had positive stories, the game would just be a collage of unicorns and rainbows.

It is the negative stories that create the backdrop for the drama.

Our minds are incredibly creative. If the mind could be trained to be as creative with wonderful tales of love, romance, and abundance as it is with our doomsday scenarios, how might that affect our experience?

MEMORY THOUGHTS

Much of what we consider thinking is really just "memory thought." Memories often come up in the mind as if to give context to what is happening in the present. Memory thoughts can often come out of the blue and seem to have nothing to do with what is actually happening in the moment.

When memory thoughts arise to make sense of what is happening now, we are basing our "now" experience on the past to give it context. This is limiting.

Have you ever traveled with someone, and every new thing that you saw, this person had to relate it to something "back home"? This is memory thought trying to give context to what is happening now. Rather than just experiencing the new, the memory mind feels the need to compare and provide context and narration from the past.

We bring this up because when you really start to observe your own thoughts, you may be surprised by how many of them are memory thoughts.

NO THOUGHT

We often hear our Buddhist friends advocating 'no thought.' This is what the goal of meditation is said to be: to empty the mind of thoughts. But if you have ever sat down to try meditation, you will notice that you are thinking about meditating, then you are thinking about having no thoughts, and then the thoughts come up, and you berate them and yourself for your inability to not think. Sounds incredibly relaxing.

Then we read somewhere that no thought is actually the space *between* thoughts. So, we sit down to meditate again and think about the space between thoughts for a while.

What they are trying to describe is the 'observer' of the thoughts, but this is terribly difficult to communicate, especially to a society that has the attention span of a gnat.

Most people have actually experienced what the 'no thought' folks are trying to describe; they just don't know it.

Perhaps a good example would be when you're really 'in the flow' of a hobby or craft that you enjoy. When you are in flow, thought isn't necessary, nor does it arise except when needed for the next step of the process. When you're in this state, thinking itself isn't necessary, only the thoughts that arise for the purpose of furthering the project.

This is the no thought state that people all over the world are sitting on their asses in meditation trying to reach, and most never make it.

How much more useful would it be to tell people to go do something they really enjoy?

INTUITIVE THOUGHTS

When we are in this 'flow' state, we are listening to our intuition. Intuitive thoughts are simply instructions. This state of functioning is, in our view, the natural state of a fully developed adult.

We all have experience with what we call 'intuition.' A thought arises that indicates something you should do; there is no judgment, and thinking is not required—you just do it. Or the answer to a problem suddenly appears in your mind out of nowhere.

This type of functioning does not require thinking. When operating from this state of flow, intuition is clearly heard, and indicated action is simply taken.

The character's act of thinking is neither present nor necessary to function.

This is where the true creative process lives, in this state of flow. Intuition is always available to us and is speaking to us. Most of us are just too caught up in repetitive thoughts to hear it. When we're in this state, we get more done with less effort, and everything becomes smooth and much less dramatic.

It can be hard to believe for someone stuck in the monkey mind that thinking is not useful or necessary to live life, but this can be experienced directly.

LEFT BRAIN VS. RIGHT BRAIN

We find it interesting to look at what our science friends think about how our brain works with regard to the way we think.

We've all heard about the left brain and the right brain, and we may have varying beliefs around the topic, such as "right-brained people are more creative."

We aren't really looking at this to uphold any of these beliefs; we are just looking with interest at what we are told that each side of the brain does.

Left side: Logic, sequencing, linear thinking, mathematics, facts, thinking in words.

Right side: Imagination, holistic thinking, intuition, arts, rhythm, nonverbal cues, feelings, visualization, daydreaming.

Have you ever observed in yourself whether you tend to think in words or in pictures?

Do you notice that there seems to be a narrator and labeler in your head that constantly tries to explain everything you experience?

If you don't have this narrator, how would you characterize your own thoughts? Are they visual?

Could it be that when we are in the 'flow' or in the 'no thought' state that meditation tries to bring about, what we are experiencing is the right brain's expansiveness and the left brain is quiet and resting until it gets its cue from the right brain when the next instructional thought is required for the next step of whatever process we are in? We don't know. We just like playing with ideas.

These types of ideas can help us when we begin to observe our own thoughts and how those thoughts work within ourselves.

THOUGHTS BECOME THINGS

While the origin of thought cannot be known, the results of thought are always on display. Nothing exists without the thought of it first. Everything that we 'see' in our world originated with a thought.

Every invention, piece of art, building, the book you're reading right now, cars, airplanes, Sunseeds, phones, etc., all began as a thought. Thoughts become things.

Thoughts are information and create everything we believe about everything. Ponder this: the origin of thought cannot be known, yet those thoughts of unknown origin create our entire experience of what we call ourselves. That's a sobering thought.

Thoughts create beliefs, emotions, perceptions, and ideas, and yet no one knows where they come from. This is an important concept to grasp before we move on; thought is really the basis of everything that we think we are.

Thoughts are the base programming of the game.

Thought is the creative power of our perceived reality. With this in mind, it is of utmost importance to observe our thoughts and the way we use the thinking faculty. As Einstein supposedly said, you can't solve a problem with the same kind of thinking that we used to create it.

So, if we are serious about changing our life experience, we must think differently. We can't begin to think differently or possibly hope to live in flow if we don't observe our mind and our habitual thinking patterns and break our addiction to them.

When you begin to get the hang of observing your thoughts, you can then begin to ponder just who this 'observer' is.

MIND DOJO

MIND DOJO

Breathing

It has long been taught that focusing on your breath can be helpful to "quiet the mind." Focusing on your breath gives your mind something else to focus on, just as a pacifier quiets a crying baby. The mind runs wild until you bring it under control. Focusing on your breath is one way to distract the mind so that you can get a good look at it and know the difference between racing thoughts and slower "purposeful" thoughts.

There are many techniques out there, but for our purposes here, let's use a very simple method.

1. Inhale through your nose.
2. Exhale through your mouth.
3. Inhale again and focus on filling your belly with air first, then move up to the lungs.
4. Exhale through your mouth.
5. Continue breathing deeply and count to four on the inhale, hold it for four counts, and count to four on the exhale.

You may feel a little more relaxed, but that's not our purpose. What did you observe in your mind? Did you have thoughts trying to come in and disrupt you? Did you wonder if you left the stove on or if you took the trash out? Did your mind make up a doomsday scenario about the dangers of breathing?

Simply observe the way your mind reacts when you are attempting to "control" it.

Observing

Try to remember this little trick throughout the day. You will need to be vigilant in watching your thoughts to even notice them.

When you do notice them, ask yourself:

- What are they imagining or saying?
- What path are they going down?
- Are they random?
- Are they spinning a scenario based on a past experience?

When you're observing your thoughts, sometimes they slow down or even stop, like when you catch a three-year-old drawing on the wall.

The observation is enough to stop them, as if they don't want to be looked at too closely.

Just notice your own mind and how the thoughts arise and what they do. Are they purposeful or useless? Are they patterned? Are they judgmental?

Just observe.

The Candle Flame

One of the exercises that we found helpful when we were getting a handle on learning how to observe our thoughts was the candle flame exercise.

Create a space that is quiet, with the least possibility of interruption or distraction. This means no phones, no music, no anything—just quiet, alone, and without distraction.

Light a candle. Sit comfortably and simply stare at the flame, focusing all of your attention on it. Can you lose yourself in the flame?

Observe what happens in your mind. How long were you able to focus on just the flame? Did random thoughts come in? Did they start out having something to do with the candle or the flame?

This is an excellent practice to begin learning to focus your attention and observe your thoughts.

Do Something That You Enjoy

Whatever you find pleasing and enjoyable—a hobby, a craft, a sport—do it.

Try to observe your thoughts during these activities. You may find this the hardest exercise because when you are in joy, you may not have many thoughts at all to observe. You may also find that attempting to observe takes you out of the flow of the activity.

Get to know these states; flow is the natural state that we want, so by observing, you will also know when you're out of it.

BELIEFS

The construct of our belief systems is so intricate that we don't even realize that most of what we 'know' is really just a belief.

Belief is the engine that drives us. Belief is how we experience the duality of the playing field and makes up most of the character structure that we use to play the game.

A belief is not based on any fact. It is a thought or a concept that you have accepted to be true. That doesn't make it true in fact; it just makes it true to you. Habitual thoughts can turn into beliefs simply because of the repeated pattern of them.

For instance, when you're a child, you receive repeated messaging.

Let's pretend that in your childhood home, you were told that the only way to grow up big and strong was to drink your own pee. Every night before bed, you had to drink a shot of your own pee while listening to your parents tell you that this was really the only way to grow strong and healthy.

You now have a belief based on repetitive messaging, so you continue drinking your own pee well into adulthood. Even though the original message was to do it to grow up big and strong, once you are grown up big and strong, it should be okay for you not to do this. But you don't put that together; it's just become a belief that this is what you must do for your overall well-being. Sure, this example is a little extreme, but we're trying to make a point.

Repetitive messaging is all around you, all the time. It's in our advertising, educational institutions, governments, religions, and our childhood homes. This repetitive messaging manipulates your thought patterns to create belief within you.

You are being manipulated by this tactic constantly. It's along the lines of telling a lie often enough that people believe it's true. It's one of the core principles of indoctrination: repeat the desired message until it solidifies as belief.

This is the 'external' input that we interpret internally and then build the character-belief around. Then the Ego takes that internal interpretation as guidance and faithfully projects it out into your external reality for you to experience.

This is super important to understand. Your beliefs will project out and create your perceived life experience.

Have you ever sat down and taken an inventory of all your beliefs and questioned where they came from? We aren't just talking about spiritual beliefs; that's just the easy, low-hanging fruit to start with.

We want you to consider ALL your beliefs.

The majority of our beliefs do not come organically from ourselves. When we're babies, we show up without beliefs. Then we are raised by people who imprint their beliefs onto our little sponge-like minds. They are only teaching what they were taught to believe from their parents and so on. But in this society, it isn't just the people who raise us that imprint beliefs; we also have our 'institutions' that get in the game to teach us what to believe.

Our minds are in such a state of suggestibility when we are young that we basically believe whatever has been imprinted. Children don't believe in Santa Claus unless the parents, advertisers, and institutions tell them about this fantastic character who will indeed judge them based on how they behave and either reward or punish them at Christmas.

If that message were not present, children would have no grounds to believe in it.

The same is true for a myriad of other messages that we receive as children. Our beliefs about money, our worldview, political views, moral codes, religious and spiritual beliefs, cultural beliefs, social issue beliefs, and especially what we believe about ourselves are imprinted on our minds as children.

About the time that we start seriously questioning our belief in Santa Claus should be about the time that we begin questioning everything else.

If our parents lied about Santa, how can we possibly trust any of the other things that we believe to be true from their imprint?

This is why questioning what beliefs you have NOW is so important. You may think that your beliefs are well thought out and based on facts, but if you've never questioned them, how would you know?

When we don't question ourselves honestly, we are running on someone else's program, and we don't develop into adults. We stay in our imprinted child mind for the rest of our years here. This is *most* people and possibly *even you*.

Here's a fun, easy example of a belief generated in childhood and carried forward through our supposed adulthood.

Little Johnny is 9 years old. He's watching his mom prepare a ham for Christmas. His mom cuts both ends off the ham before putting it in the pan.

Johnny asks, "Mom, why do you cut the ends off the ham?" His mom answers, "Because it makes it taste better."

This is perplexing to Johnny, so further inquiry is needed. "But how does that make it taste better?" Mom is now a little irritated, "Because it just does."

Johnny is not so easily put off. "I still don't see how that would make it taste better."

Mom answers with exasperation, "I learned it from your grandma, go ask her."

So, Johnny seeks out grandma with his drive to get to the bottom of this.

He asks, "Grandma, how does cutting the ends off the ham make it taste better?"

Grandma is perplexed by this out-of-the-blue question and needs clarification. "What do you mean? Who says it makes it taste better?"

Johnny responds, "Mom said that it makes it taste better and that you always did it so you would know why."

Grandma laughs so hard she has tears flowing down her cheeks.

When she catches her breath, she replies, "I cut the ends off my ham because I never had a pan big enough to fit the whole thing."

This is exactly what we do: we take things that we see or hear as children and then create a story around them. Johnny's mom has been wasting ham for years because it never occurred to her to question why she was cutting the ends off. She assumed that it had something to do with the taste.

Here's another fun example from a friend of ours named Cheri. When Cheri was 13, a new girl came to her school. Her name was Tammy. Tammy was from California; she was 14 and extremely large-breasted for any age, much less 14. Tammy also wore full-blown makeup and was the absolute coolest person Cheri had ever met.

One day, Tammy told Cheri that the reason boys liked her was that she did her eye makeup using three different types of mascara. So, Cheri naturally believed that she also needed three different types of mascara and used these three different types for years.

It wasn't until much later that Cheri even realized she was still doing her makeup on the advice of a 14-year-old girl who actually thought that male attention was the result of mascara and not her double-D breast size. We aren't sure what happened to Tammy, but we can imagine that she figured out soon enough that it wasn't the mascara after all.

As adults, we should have honed our sword of discernment, but most of us never do.

We take what we've been told by others and accept it as fact.

When we don't question what we have believed from childhood, this type of passivity spills over into our adult lives.

THE PLACEBO EFFECT

Beliefs are some of the most powerful things in our experience. The placebo effect is a great example of this because most people are familiar with it.

The placebo effect, to put it simply, is that your *belief in* the medicine is as strong or, in some cases, stronger than the medicine itself.

Conditioning is a facet of this phenomenon; this is when you form an association between two things, resulting in a learned response.

An example of this would be if you regularly take medication for arthritis that gives you relief from pain. If you're given a pill that looks the same as your regular medication but is actually a placebo, you may still get the same pain relief.

Expectation, or *what we believe we will experience*, plays a significant role in the placebo effect.

If this is the case, then if we believed strongly enough that we had the capacity to heal ourselves through our thoughts, as some folks do, with this placebo effect in mind, that idea becomes an incredibly reasonable conclusion.

We also see the opposite effect of our beliefs with regard to medicine when a patient is given a placebo but then experiences side effects associated with the actual medicine. This is called the 'nocebo effect.'

Our minds are incredibly powerful, and our bodies follow the mind. Consider how much sickness we are creating simply by believing in sickness every day. Looking up symptoms on Google is not your friend. Your mind can and will create sickness if you believe in it strongly enough. This is the 'nocebo effect' without being given anything but a belief.

This is mind-blowing stuff and should give you pause. Your beliefs are so incredibly powerful that questioning and finding out where the beliefs come from should be included in the safety manual of life. Beliefs are weapons of mass construction and destruction and should never, ever be taken lightly.

When you begin to seriously question your beliefs, you will soon find that they are all built on sand and none of them are true. Remember, 'true to you' does not and cannot count as actual truth.

If beliefs were set in stone and founded on truth, it would be impossible for us to change our minds about anything.

No belief is true.

BELIEF IS THE FOUNDATION OF THE EGO-CHARACTER

Our entire character structure is built on belief. The things that we believe deeply about ourselves—so deeply that we don't even know they are there anymore—are what cling to the structure of the Ego. Our character begins to structure itself in childhood, and that structure solidifies over time.

Let's say that you grew up in a household where you heard the phrase "You should be ashamed of yourself!" repeated over and over again. This creates a little seed of belief within you. That seed begins to grow like vines around the Ego-trellis within you. This is now part of your 'character.' There is so much emotion generated by, and attached to, this belief that you should be ashamed that you eventually do become ashamed of yourself.

If shame is your core belief, then the life that you create will be one to be ashamed of.

The shame vines will suffocate even the positive things that you may have heard from your parents. Most of us will remember the 'shame' messaging, but we don't remember the praise.

In fact, the shame vine is so prevalent that it may even make you ashamed of the wonderful things that you have done, created, or accomplished. We see this a lot in imposter syndrome when you don't feel worthy of your own accomplishments. We don't recognize it for what it is: a belief that we should be ashamed of ourselves.

Let's say that you grew up in a household where your parents routinely made comments like, "We can't afford that," or "That's too expensive," "What do you think, money grows on trees?"

Because, in childhood, you are an extension of your parents, this too is a little seed of belief that begins to grow within. You will most likely create a life that doesn't provide quite enough money. There is always lack and struggle. You must work hard just to get by.

These types of beliefs that grow in childhood can, and in most cases do, limit you to a life lived within their boundaries.

JUDGMENT

Beliefs are the base camp of judgment.

Our beliefs are the structure of the character, which provides it with its basis for judgment. This is really the main thing the character does: it judges constantly. It can't judge anything as good, bad, right, or wrong without the underlying belief structure in place.

The character judges the self and others against this belief spectrum.

All experience is neutral; it is your judgment that makes the experience good or bad.

We're not criticizing the character here; the character is necessary to varying degrees within this game.

We're just pointing out that most of what it does is judge. Judgment is its job.

These belief and judgment filters are how we perceive the world. We judge everything and everyone, and most of all, ourselves.

Then we have the emotional component. It's important to notice how much emotional focus we invest in our beliefs.

Why are we afraid to question our own beliefs?

When someone else questions our beliefs about something, we feel attacked or offended, and that emotional reaction really gets us going. Emotion is the immediate response within the body to a perceived threat, and then we label that emotion as a feeling, so now we have both the body and the mind perceiving a threat.

Everyone reacts differently to threats because everyone perceives them differently. It is very telling that the bodily emotion would perceive a belief being questioned as a valid, *physical* threat. Who or what is being threatened by a question?

When we begin to seriously question our beliefs, we naturally also question our judgment. When this really gets going and you're questioning some deep core beliefs, it can feel like a dismantling of self. Because in a way, it is. This is the dismantling of the structure that you've believed was you.

When we don't question these very core beliefs, we continue to be limited by them.

As we've pointed out, beliefs are made from thoughts that we focus on until they seem true.

When we are in the 'thinking' stage, the thoughts are just passing fancies, but when we think them repeatedly over a period of time, they begin to solidify into belief. When we're still in the thinking mode before a belief has been solidified, we don't get offended at someone questioning the thought.

It's when the thoughts have solidified into belief that the character feels the need to defend it. Thoughts can be questioned, but beliefs are sacred ground and must be defended.

This is like saying we can question the freshness of the eggs used to bake a cake, but we cannot question the freshness of the cake once it's baked.

So, our equation of this character built around the Ego structure is this:

Thought creates Belief. Belief creates Judgment. Judgment creates Emotion.

That's the never-ending feedback loop that most of us operate from.

We have a thought that we habitually think. It most likely isn't our thought but something someone else told us, so it's someone else's thought. This creates a belief that the thought(s) must be true. This is the basis for our judgment of everything that we see as either right or wrong, good or bad. When we are presented with something that we have judged to be wrong or bad based on our belief, we then have the feelings attached to it. These feelings would naturally be along the spectrum of anger, indignation, sadness, grief, shame, or rage.

The same is true if we are presented with something that we've judged to be right or good. Then the feelings are along the range of happiness, excitement, affection, or contentment.

We live our lives on this emotional roller coaster fueled by thought and belief. This is what we're using to create our experience in the game: thoughts, beliefs, judgment, and emotion. If these things are responsible for our entire experience on the playing field of this game, wouldn't they be the things we would want to dissect and get to the bottom of so that we could have an optimal game experience?

An example of this thought-belief-judgment-emotion roller coaster might look something like this:

You had repetitive messaging as a child that being even a little bit chubby was unacceptable. So, you grew up with this belief as a part of your character, and now as an adult, you still hold on to the idea that fat is bad, wrong or unacceptable. Your character sees overweight people and immediately judges them as 'less than' or 'not acceptable' in some way. This does two things: it makes others 'wrong' or 'less than' and it makes the character 'right' or 'better than' others. This is almost an automatic function every time you see an overweight person.

Then, you reach an age where your hormones go crazy. You begin to put on weight that you cannot lose, no matter what you do. Now we have the character judging *itself* as 'not acceptable,' and some serious negative self-talk can arise. We berate ourselves, call ourselves names, call ourselves weak, and our emotions get involved. We then feel weak, ashamed, guilty, or flawed in some way. But even with this kind of self-judgment, when we walk down the street and see another overweight person, the judgment is again turned 'outward,' and it may sound something like this: "Well, I'm overweight, but at least I'm not as overweight as that other person."

This again keeps the character feeling 'better than' others, but still judging itself as 'not good enough.'

This is the roller coaster where most folks spend their lives, and if we don't look at it, it will continue unabated.

This is why we must be willing to question every belief that we have if we want to have a different experience. We have to stop being afraid of the questions and create space for the answers to these questions to arise.

Sadly, these things are so intricate and ingrained in us that we have been mistaking them for who we are. Our entire persona is built on things that we haven't questioned and can't possibly know if any of them are true.

We are building our entire identity around lies and deception.

That last sentence may have triggered an emotional response within you, probably along the lines of righteous indignation. "I am NOT a lie! That's horseshit! I know exactly who I am."

That's what the character does. It will do anything to protect itself because the act of inspecting the foundations of what the character is made of is a major threat, and defense is necessary. If you keep going, you'll have an all-out war on your hands. The character does not like to lose, and it will fight for its existence. It has been running the show, and when you question its authority to do so, you become the usurper.

This sounds like bloody awful business, and it is. We have given our power over to a construct of beliefs, and the character rules that domain. It's all fluff masquerading as solid rock.

Again, we're not dogging on the character. It's important in this game, and it fuels the most magnificent drama. How boring would this game be without drama? Ego is the gift that keeps on giving within the game because it faithfully carries out the commands of the character. We just want to convey the information that may be helpful for playing the game differently, and understanding Ego and character is paramount to having a different experience.

THE HOUSE WE LIVE IN

Whose house do you live in? If our base character structure is comprised mostly of hand-me-down beliefs, how can we say it's really ours?

It's like living in a house filled with all the stuff from every generation that has previously lived there. You move in and bring your few belongings with you, but all the other old, outdated garbage is there too. This house has never had any trash service, so the trash just continues to pile up. You've got stuff from your great-great-great-grandmother in there that you don't even know about. This house is a hoarder's paradise.

Generation after generation, no one has seen the need to call the trash man and have it taken away. It's been there so long that we become emotionally attached to it. The house is super confining, and we can't move around easily, but it's all we know. We can't even get an accurate floor plan of the house and have no idea how large it is because it's so full of crap.

Some of the rooms aren't even rooms; they're just pathways between the trash, but we can't see it, and so we stay comfortably in the rooms with walls built out of crap. We just redecorate the walls with our own childish finger paintings to make it more "ours."

It doesn't occur to us to take out the trash because we don't see it as trash; we see it as truth.

This is exactly where many humans live. Most are still just children believing they are adults, but they have never taken the developmental journey to become adults.

Wouldn't you rather live in a house that YOU designed, one that no one else has lived in?

If we are to develop out of childhood into adulthood, we must take out the trash. YOU must be the trash man. The trash man is the hero of our story. You cannot begin to design your own house until you can find the door to get out of your current hoarder haven. You can't find the door until you take out the trash.

We will say here that if you are content with your current dwelling, then stay. If you are content being a child in a world designed for children, there's nothing wrong with that.

If you would like to naturally develop into an adult and view the world from that perspective, then you'll have to do the work of the trash man.

Simple as that.

Be forewarned, it isn't pleasant, and if you complete the task, your life will not be the same.

You'll view the world as a child's birthday party at a Chuck E. Cheese restaurant, and you're the only adult in attendance.

But at least you will be living in a structure that you built and not stuck in the putrid stench of unquestioned beliefs.

MIND DOJO

MIND DOJO

Questioning Beliefs

WARNING:

Once you sincerely begin this process, it will be difficult, if not impossible, to go back to your 'old' way of life.

You should make this choice wisely and with clear intent. It is extremely likely that when you begin to shine a serious light on your beliefs, your life will never be the same.

In light of this, we encourage you to dip your toe into this practice with some of your non-threatening, softball beliefs first.

Take just one thing that you believe to be true. Perhaps a belief that you were taught in childhood that you still hold on to but aren't quite sure why.

For instance:

> **I have been drinking a shot of my own pee every night before bed for my entire life.**

- Where did this come from?
- What is the earliest I can remember this?
- Is it true that it is the only way to ensure health?

or

I believe that eating meat is unhealthy.

- Where did this come from?
- What is the earliest I can remember this belief?
- Do I have a full spectrum of information to either confirm or disprove this belief?
- Where does the information come from?
- Is the source actually reliable?
- What if the information I found was all funded by plant-based companies?
- Is that reliable?
- Have I looked up, read, and understood all the significant studies on this subject?
- Are there significant independently funded studies on this subject?
- Did my information come from an ad campaign?
- Do I know others who eat meat that are healthy?
- Do I know people who do not eat meat that are unhealthy?
- Why exactly is meat unhealthy?
- How did people eat meat for thousands of years if it is so unhealthy?
- What if I abandon this belief? How would my life change?
- What if I just abandon the need for this belief and am no longer attached to it?

We suggest that you take just a few of these beliefs, follow this template of questioning, and write down your observations. Get the information out of your head and onto a piece of paper so you can look at it.

Book three of the Sacred Series,

Lenswork: The Sacred Work of Self-Destruction,

has some helpful drills in Phase 1 for this kind of belief inquiry. Phase 1 of that book would most likely be beneficial for most folks.

Don't worry, Phase 1 is just a little deeper dive into belief questioning; you won't burst into the awakened no-self.

You could do Phase 1 and stop. It would give you a much clearer framework to dissect your structural beliefs.

Happy Hunting!

EMOTIONS AND FEELINGS

Emotions have a big part to play in our Ego-character/structure. They are the 'glue' that binds all the rest together. Emotions hold the beliefs and judgments of the character tightly to the Ego frame.

No one can tell us exactly what emotions are or how they work. There are tons of theories, and some of them seem to make sense, but emotions are truly one of those mysterious things that we all experience yet have no idea how they work.

In the 1970s, psychologist Paul Ekman identified six basic emotions that he suggested were universally experienced in all human cultures. The "basic" emotions he identified were happiness, sadness, disgust, fear, surprise, and anger. He later expanded his list of basic emotions to include pride, shame, embarrassment, and excitement.

Dr. Eckman's definition of emotions:

"Emotions are a process, a particular kind of automatic appraisal influenced by our evolutionary and personal past, in which we sense that something important to our welfare is occurring, and a set of psychological changes and emotional behaviors begins to deal with the situation."

In other words, emotions are unbidden responses; they happen before we think about them as a reaction to something perceived as important. Dr. Eckman also says that all emotions vary in their onset and decline, but generally do not last more than an hour. If an emotion lasts for an extended amount of time without interruption, he categorizes those as a mood or a disorder.

It is very telling that in Dr. Eckman's definition of emotions, he uses the term 'emotional behaviors.' Words are often limiting when we are trying to describe the indescribable. It's also important to note that the science guys differentiate between emotions and feelings. In their world, emotions are more of a physical, unbidden response, and feelings fall somewhere under the umbrella of thought.

This is an interesting concept to explore as it relates to our character structure. The emotional and feeling differences look something like this:

Let's say you are driving home, and a car pulls out in front of you. You slam on the brakes and narrowly avoid a terrible accident. Emotion arises as fear, and the body reacts to the situation. Maybe you get the shakes and need to pull over until everything calms down. The emotion of fear dissipates naturally because it is no longer needed to deal with the immediate situation.

As you sit there pulled over, the thought construct comes out to play. Now maybe you have feelings of gratitude that you avoided the accident; maybe you even say a prayer of thanks to something outside of yourself. Then, after the "whew! I'm lucky to be alive" feeling dissipates, the feeling of anger may come in. Anger at the other driver, anger that someone else put your life in danger, anger that other people are allowed to drive at all when they clearly don't know what they're doing.

Now you're completing your trip home, stewing with anger but also ever watchful for other assholes on the road. By the time you get home, you have an extremely compelling story to tell, complete with a villain, a victim, and an unknown saving grace that protected you. You spend the next two hours ruminating on all these feelings and reliving the experience by telling anyone who will listen.

Your thoughts are now keeping the feelings going while the emotion has long since dissipated because the body knows there is no danger in the moment. The thoughts and feelings are fueling the dramatic experience of the character construct. Drama is somewhat of an addiction that feeds itself; it fuels self-importance, which is one of the things that keeps the character intact and gives it the illusion of control at all times. The addiction to this drama would be evident when you continue to tell the story to your friends for the next two weeks.

If you're one of those people who downloaded a 'mindfulness' app, as soon as you got done telling your story for a couple of hours, you would need to go into the app and log your feelings, track your triggers, and then get the 'mindfulness' community on the app to weigh in on your experience. This way, you get your feelings and your triggers validated, which also keeps them very much alive and operating within you.

If you have one of these apps, do yourself a favor: cancel your subscription and delete it. The only thing that these types of apps do is keep you in your victimhood, which you get to collectively celebrate with others. The character loves this; the app developers do too and would love for you to continue to pay your monthly subscription to stay safely under the character's thumb.

For simplicity's purposes, we will be using "emotion" and "feeling" as the same thing. We aren't science guys, and our common language doesn't differentiate between the two.

Emotions are such a large part of our human experience and create the dramatic tapestry of our lives.

They are how we experience being in love, the excitement of the days leading up to Christmas, or being angry with your family, which leads you to skip Christmas and feel lonely. Emotions are what give us such a wide range of experience in this dualistic playing field.

It is very telling that we feel the need to not only label these emotions but also judge them to be positive or negative. Emotions and feelings are simply vehicles with which we experience the game, but we have made even these natural, experiential elements of our lives either good or bad, desired or undesired, better or worse. We fail to see that without the 'negative' feelings, 'positive' feelings would not be possible. There would be nothing to compare them with.

We often make the distinction between 'emotional' thinking and 'logical' thinking. Emotions can cloud the mind and our judgment. On the flip side, if we are only logical and deny or suppress emotions, we shortchange ourselves in the experience realm.

All feelings are attachments. It's like they are made of sticky spider web material and cling to everything. Emotional bonding is what attaches us to our families and loved ones. This kind of bonding is a basic human need. However, this emotional bonding can also become exceedingly limiting and keep us living in unhealthy situations.

Emotions and feelings attach us to our beliefs. When our beliefs are questioned, our emotions provide the fuel for us to feel the need to defend and justify those beliefs. If we were not emotionally attached to our beliefs, we would release any belief with ease and with no more thought than throwing away an old, worn-out T-shirt.

We are emotionally invested in propping up our beliefs because emotions are the fuel and the glue for the character structure. Who would we be without our emotional investment in our 'identity'? In the context of our character structure, no belief would survive if there were no emotion to fuel its defense.

All emotions and feelings are a natural part of our experiential game and have their rightful place within us. It is when we exalt emotions to a higher importance than they have or suppress emotions to a lesser importance than is natural that we get into trouble. Emotions and feelings are there to be felt—not worshiped, not held onto, not suppressed, or ignored; they are meant to be felt and then let go. This is the healthy, rightful place of emotions, providing feelings and experiences but not ruling our lives.

Our feelings and emotions are an important part of our navigational system, and when we don't have a holistic understanding of them, we can quickly get off track.

When we stay in our 'heads' and don't give emotions and feelings the space to arise, flow through, and dissipate from our bodies, the energy gets stuck. Our bodies, in a very real way, are the physical representation of the flow or blockage of our emotional energy.

When we judge certain emotions to be negative, unacceptable, or undesirable, we tend to 'shove them down' and not allow the free expression of those feelings.

For instance, if we were raised in an environment where anger was not allowed to be expressed, then, out of our survival instinct, we learned to shove anger down. A likely outcome of this could be unexplained pain and stiffness in the body, which could possibly lead to disease. The angry emotions get 'stuck' and never properly move through the nervous system.

This is not only detrimental to the body but also to our ability to fully feel other emotions.

The mind-body connection with regard to emotions can't be overstated. Emotions need to be felt; the energy needs to move through the nervous system and, most importantly, be released. If the energy doesn't move, it can't be released. We end up with a very unregulated nervous system and a diminished capacity to fully feel our lives.

It may also lead us to hate our bodies because the body holds the unexpressed secrets.

There is also the opposite end of the spectrum when our emotions run wild. When we allow our emotions or feelings to run our lives without a proper understanding of their rightful place, we limit our experience of life.

When we find ourselves in this 'emotional' functioning most of the time, the energy isn't getting properly released from the nervous system either. The mind and the body create a feedback loop for one another, and so the emotions just keep circulating. There is no room for clear thinking or intuition to appear when we are in this state.

In our current society, we have placed emotions and feelings on the throne, and they rule the world. We have also divested ourselves of any responsibility for our own feelings, making us victims of them.

Emotions are the currency of our undeveloped human society. You are sold on emotion, you vote on emotion, you support or boycott on emotion, you spend your time and money on emotion, and you interact with people on emotion. This society preys on and uses your emotions to drive sales and agendas.

Social media is a mega cult of emotional reactions. Body shaming, cyberbullying, revenge porn, political rants, fake backgrounds, photo filters, fake money, fake cars, fake millionaires, fake courses, fake spirituality, and all the rest of the dazzling display of horse shit is designed to engage you and *keep* you engaged emotionally. How much of your life force are you putting into this nonsense? Do you even *know* that you are being manipulated?

We've seen this kind of emotional manipulation ratcheted up in the last few years; it's everywhere you look. It causes division and defensive posturing; it creates a language of vitriol that masquerades as reasonable discourse. When one event or issue has run out of emotional steam, another one pops up immediately to take its place, and then tens of millions of people are rushing to change their profile picture on social media to show their support or opposition to the emotional trigger of the month.

Families are divided, and friends no longer speak to one another over this kind of emotional manipulation. There is no such thing as honest intellectual debate any longer; there is no room for simple disagreement; it's our way or the highway. Emotions have overthrown the governing intellect.

This kind of over-emotional functioning is, in our view, the reason so many folks feel like they are 'suffering.'

Emotions and feelings do not cause suffering on their own. It is our resistance to the emotions and feelings that causes our pain and emotional suffering.

When we are resisting emotions, we are also resisting what is. We are in resistance to our 'reality.'

Anytime you find yourself fighting something, you are in resistance. Even if the enemy you're fighting is something that sounds righteous, like 'social justice,' it is still resistance to what is. These kinds of wars will never be won. Just as we see when our government deploys something like the 'war on drugs,' when we fight something, the problem generally gets bigger.

Anytime we are trying to exert control over the 'external', we are in resistance to it, and our desired change will not solidify; we can only receive more resistance reflecting back to us. The only real change that can come about is when we surrender and accept what is, and then do the work to change the 'internal', because that is where dissatisfaction and suffering have their origin.

Resistance will always cause suffering, and the more you resist, the worse it will be.

When we are in resistance to our emotions and feelings, there is a 'war' within. To get the peace we say we want, we can't continue to resist. We must accept and allow the feelings and emotions to be fully felt and released. If we don't allow ourselves to feel them, we are in resistance to what is. If we hold onto them, we are in resistance to the release.

Emotions and feelings should be accepted, felt, and released.

When we resist any part of this process, it will cause suffering.

Emotions tell us that our beliefs and opinions are our identity, and they must be defended at all costs.

The energy generated by our emotions is the tie that binds the entire character structure together. We spend an incredible amount of our life force propping up our character AS our identity. If we removed the emotional fuel, it would crumble like the house of cards that it is.

From our view, all emotions are really just fear wearing a brilliant costume. As we go through this process of dissecting our beliefs and our character structure, we have come to realize that everything is based on fear. Fear is the emotion that fuels us.

What we call love in modern society is just a puppet with fear's hand up its ass. We fear losing love more than we actually love because losing love would be a direct hit to our character identity.

Even when we are experiencing happiness, there is the whisper of fear that it won't last. This is why we adopt the 'enjoy it while it lasts' attitude because we fear that it won't.

Fear can be found in everything. It is pervasive. This is because the character knows that it is just a fabrication, and so the greatest fear is the fear of nonexistence. This is the base emotion of the character because it lives in an illusion of separation, knowing itself to be a false construct.

The 'you' that you really are is not the character identity that has been constructed. Emotions and feelings are what attach you to the belief that your character identity is who you are.

This is SELF-Deception and it's how the game is played.

We have deceived ourselves into the belief that we are the avatar within the game; how else could the programmer of the game have a wonderful, dramatic experience? It's necessary to program the self-deception into the game itself; otherwise, the programmer couldn't play the game with limitations. Without this element, the programmer would always be in 'god mode' in the game, and that's only fun for a few minutes. The limitations created by self-deception are necessary for the dramatic elements to feel real.

In other words:

The 'you' that you think you are, is a fictional character and doesn't exist. It is only a thought construct that you *believe* is 'you'.

In the next section, we will do our best to give you some representations of how we experience this remarkable character structure.

MIND DOJO

MIND DOJO

Questions to Ponder

Think of a recent event that you got emotional about.

It doesn't matter if you thought it was positive or negative, just an event that elicited a strong emotional response.

- What feelings did you experience?
- If the event was judged to be negative, what were the core feelings surrounding it?
- Did you feel unsafe, threatened, disrespected, etc.?
- What belief was this reaction attached to?
- Do the same exercise if the event was positive.
- How did the event make you feel?
- What belief was this emotion attached to?
- Were you able to experience the feelings and emotions and then let them go?
- Did you ruminate on the event, and so the emotions were brought up over and over again?

We are just sharpening our swords of curiosity here. Begin to look at emotional reactions and feelings and dissect them.

We encourage you to drill down on the emotion or feeling.

Don't just cop out and say, "it made me feel sad." Why did it make you feel sad?

Is there something else within the sadness, like other feelings?

Really drill down on this. You're getting to know yourself, and you are a fabulously interesting character, so make it fun.

THE DOME CONCEPT

Now that we've looked at the Ego-character structure, let's examine how this shows up in the game of life.

Here's a fun example of how we create the character structure in our lives:

You're a toddler riding in the basket of a shopping cart, and as you're being pushed around, you pull things off the shelves and surround yourself with them.

You really pile it up to the point that you can't see anything beyond what you've pulled into your cart. This is now your reality.

You're not even halfway through the store ,but you've limited your experience to the pile of crap in your cart.

You might get a glimpse through the cracks at some other really cool stuff, but you don't believe you can have it because you're full.

You would have to let go and get rid of something to make room for something else. Most people today go through their entire lives this way, with a cart full of crap that was super cool when they were children but now restricts them to a limited experience.

Another way we could explain how the character structure works in the game is with what we call the

"Dome Concept."

Your character structure of beliefs, thoughts, and judgments creates an invisible dome around your game avatar. You can move anywhere you want in the game, but the dome moves with you. You can see outside of it and see things that you would like to have, but when you step closer to what you want, the dome around you keeps that thing you don't have at the same distance away.

The entire playing field stays exactly where it is relative to your dome.

The dome is powered by a generator; the fuel for the generator is emotion and attachment. The dome requires an incredible amount of energy to keep it up, and so we are constantly fueling it with our emotions and attachments.

Fear is generally the supercharged fuel that runs the generator. Fear, masked as love, anger, self-loathing, insecurity, pride, or a host of other 'emotions,' is generally at the root of all of them.

The dome is your limit of what you can and will experience in the game. It looks like you're going to new places, but because the dome is always moving with you, your experiences are most often the same, just with different costumes and characters. The dome simply mirrors back to you your own beliefs and thoughts.

Everything that you perceive outside of you is simply a mirror image of your prevailing thoughts, beliefs, and emotions. That's why your life never really seems to change; no matter 'where' you are, 'you' are always powering the dome to mirror back to you whatever your core concepts are.

Until the core concepts change, your experience can't change.

No amount of positive affirmations, vision boards, writing in a 3, 6, 9 journal, shadow work, or repeating a mantra will make any lasting change in your life as long as your core concepts and beliefs remain unquestioned and intact. No matter how many seminars you attend or how many times you walk on hot coals, as long as the core concepts and beliefs are being fueled, there will not be any long-term change in your experience.

We spend most of our lives fueling the dome, fueling our own limitations, and then wonder why we can't seem to get anywhere.

When we don't understand the dome concept, we waste a tremendous amount of time and energy searching for something that will give us a better life, but the 'better life' cannot and will not manifest as long as your dome is intact.

This is where the spiritual mall comes in. All religions and spiritualities are designed to dangle a carrot in front of you with the promise of something better. They are also designed to keep the dome firmly in place, which means that 'something better' can never appear in your playing field.

The only way to change your experience is to begin removing the fuel from the generator and stop wasting all that life force energy on keeping the dome intact. You are only limiting yourself if you continue to pour your energy into maintaining the dome of the false self.

When we begin to remove the emotional fuel from the generator, the dome begins to crack. When the dome cracks enough, we can bust through one part of the dome, and then we find ourselves in a larger dome with more possibilities that we can reach. That's when our experience begins to change. We now have access to a larger playing field.

We can continue this process until our dome is so expansive that it doesn't feel much like a dome at all. Then the game really gets fun. Then the experience becomes one of effortless flow.

We fearlessly explore our playing field, and everything is available to us. We become the creative force we were born to be; we do big things with little effort; we become abundant rather than waiting for abundance to be 'given' to us by some force outside of ourselves.

The perceived separation between us and our environment is thinner. This is what we mean by becoming an adult.

This is the functioning of a fully developed adult human being. This is the fun stuff; this is the stuff that makes us excited to get out of bed every day.

This is also what almost no one gets to. We've lost the ability to fully develop because there aren't any actual adults to guide us through it.

There are only children masquerading as adults who have not fully developed either, and so we lose even the concept that there is more to life.

We spend our entire lives fueling our dome, staying limited and undeveloped, and thinking that we are 'grown-ups' and that's just the way life is.

Your dome is really just the larger 'womb' that you were born into. When we don't take the step of going within and building our own chrysalis, where we do the work of maturing, we are stuck in this womb dome for the rest of our days.

When we naturally develop, build our own chrysalis, dismantle the womb concepts that no longer serve us, and grow our wings, we emerge as self-born, and the dome becomes expansive. There are far fewer limits to our experience, and we can play in higher levels of the game with ease.

The dome is the obstruction of the character that keeps the effortless flow out of reach. The dome is the false separation.

If you say you want happiness, abundance, peace of mind, joy, contentment, a Ferrari, or whatever, until you dismantle your dome, these will constantly be out of reach for you.

Everything you want is waiting on the other side of the dome, but few will do the necessary work to remove the obstruction of thoughts, beliefs, and attachments to get there.

The Ego-character has a rightful place in our experience. When we are in our limited, womb-like dome, the character is fully in charge, doing a job that it isn't qualified for. It wasn't designed to run the show.

The rightful place of the character is to navigate based on instructions from the programmer or player. The character only has the capacity to run a pre-set program. It isn't designed to make decisions; it only runs a program. Like a record, the grooves are set, and so it plays the same thing over and over again. Without proper instruction, it just does what it's always done: create the same experience over and over based on the beliefs at its structural core.

When we develop into adulthood, the Ego-character takes a seat and waits for instruction, then navigates true to course. The Ego-character is an interface that can be reprogrammed to carry out the instructions of intuition. This results in a far more expansive experience—out of the merry-go-round of the dome and into the larger amusement park.

In the next section, we'll take a look at how this Ego dome limits and arrests our development in 'real life.'

THE EGO-CHARACTER DOME IN 'REAL LIFE'

The Ego-character dome (false or fictional self) only exists because we constantly prop it up. Let's look at a few examples of how this works in 'real life.'

PRODUCTIVITY

Let's say that you're a person who needs to be constantly productive. It drives you; you get up at 5 a.m. so that you can jam more time into the day to be productive. You get an almost orgasmic satisfaction from marking things off your 'to-do' list. From the outside, you look like a powerhouse, and you're most likely respected and successful. Others look at you and think you've really got it all together.

You'll most likely rise a few rungs on the corporate ladder because whenever there's a project, you volunteer, knowing you'll get it done. You also have trouble delegating because it's just faster to do it yourself. You're a real 'do-it-yourself' kind of person. You do things for others, take care of your family, and manage scheduling and meal prepping so the week runs smoothly. You spend your weekends cleaning your house, maybe listening to music or an audiobook while you do it, and you consider that fun and relaxing.

You rarely take time to sit with yourself. Your entire existence is wrapped up in constant activity. You probably feel guilty if you get sick and can't perform to your usual standards. You may even feel guilty or selfish if you actually take a day off, so you don't. You most likely have so many plates spinning that, in your mind, if you stop for even a moment, the entire thing could crash down. You live your life dancing as fast as you can, and that kind of constant striving feels completely normal to you.

You may feel proud of your accomplishments, but we would guess that you really don't. This type of character identity needs the constant fuel of 'not enough,' so you most likely look at your accomplishments as if they are less than perfect. You probably also think that you are average, ignoring the mountain of evidence of your accomplishments that suggests you are not average but possibly extraordinary.

You don't take much time to appreciate all the things that you can do; you don't take time to appreciate yourself. You can't relax; there is an underlying shame involved in 'relaxing.'

How did you get this way? How was your character and identity built so that this was the outcome?

If we had to guess, we would say there was probably a parent with the same affliction. Perhaps you were told you were lazy as a child, or you always had a long list of chores that you had to get done, or you would be punished. Maybe you heard your parents say, "He who doesn't work, doesn't eat." Maybe it was pounded into you that to be a good citizen, you need to have a good work ethic, or to be successful and go anywhere in life, you have to work really hard at it.

It's possible that you may have been given the responsibility of raising younger siblings to some degree. Maybe you were a latchkey kid and had to take care of yourself, your siblings, and have dinner ready when your mom got home from work. Perhaps you were born into a seriously messed up environment, and so you learned to be hyper-vigilant very early on. You kept your head down as much as possible, walking on eggshells so as not to upset the powder keg environment any further.

No matter where it came from, it created a character/identity structure that you believe to be true, telling you that you have to do everything. The world will not spin if you don't. You will let everyone down. You'll lose your job, your partner, or your house if you don't keep doing what you do. While you may look like a powerhouse on the outside, on the inside and in your private life, things might be a little dicey.

This is your dome. This limits you. You believe so strongly that you have to earn your right to be here by doing everything and working hard that your reality mirrors exactly that back to you.

You create your experience of attracting people to take care of, attracting employers or jobs that require you to do more than perhaps they pay you for. You create a family that doesn't lift a finger to help around the house. If they do, you feel guilty that you didn't do it all. You'll most likely create the experience of living on the razor's edge; you may have money problems or family problems because this character identity needs crisis to avert to fuel any sense of self-worth. You will create the experience and the people in your life who require you to continue this madness.

You never ask for help; you seem strong on the outside, but it's fake. It's a lie. You create the experience of having to be in control and in constant productivity at all times because you live in fear that you are not enough. You live in fear that you are somehow not worthy of just being and that your entire self-worth relies on doing. You can't take a break, and you can't imagine any other way to live life.

You will strive and struggle to try to create a better life, but you won't achieve it. When you believe that you have to do everything, your dome is so thick that even if a million dollars were sitting right within your reach, you wouldn't be able to break through the dome to get it.

You believe that you have to earn it, and so in your reality, you will create the experience of having to earn, strive, and work hard, and never quite get there.

You can either live out the rest of your time here in this constant activity mode, or you can find what fuels this belief and begin to remove your emotional fuel from it.

We would start by identifying the underlying core concept of who you are. What is the belief that perpetuates this frantic lifestyle? Question it. Find out if it's yours. Who put it there?

If this was a message from childhood around which you've built your entire character structure, then you are living a child's life. Journaling can be very helpful with this. It's important to get the thoughts and beliefs out of your head so you can look at them with clarity. Find out what's true and expose what is not true.

Once you find the lie that this came from, you can then remove your emotional fuel from it. Without emotion to fuel it, it will cease to run your life, a crack will appear in your dome, and you can let some air in. When you bag up all the trash of this belief and throw it out, the dome cracks enough for you to walk into a much larger playing field.

This is becoming an adult. Questioning and getting to the bottom of your beliefs and understanding that they are untrue is the first step toward developing into an adult.

When you step out of your dome of productivity, you'll find that you get more done with less effort. When you are not fueling this false identity, your entire life will begin to reflect this change back to you.

Your family will help keep the house clean, your employer may give you a serious raise, and your life won't be full of crisis management, scheduling, and prepping any longer.

Rest will be a delight. Life will flow with more sweetness; you'll appreciate yourself and your accomplishments. Sounds pretty great, right?

All it takes is releasing the fear of questioning your beliefs. Then you will begin to get a glimpse of who and what you really are. The process isn't pleasant. You will have an identity crisis at first. But this is what is required to get out of your limited dome.

Most people will never take this step. But you don't have to be most people. You can be brave, take a look at what is, and stop believing what isn't.

MONEY

Maybe your struggle is with money. We've all placed money on a throne of importance due to our lack of understanding of how it flows. This is evidenced by seeing how many courses are out there to manifest more money.

Money, money, money, it's always an underlying issue, and the issue is generally fear and lack. There never seems to be enough; you constantly strive to get more, and it seems to go out faster than it comes in.

There may be multiple reasons why you have the core concept of lack or unworthiness that results in money issues.

It could be that you grew up in a home where the common themes were "we can't afford that," "rich people are greedy," "money is the root of all evil," "money doesn't grow on trees," or "eat the rich."

If these messages are present in the home, then we will naturally create a belief structure that tells us that resources are scarce or that we can't have money and be a good person at the same time, or that money is extremely hard to come by.

When we continue to fuel these beliefs, we create the experience of lack in our lives over and over again. Remember that the dome can only reflect back to you the core beliefs or concepts that you are holding on to.

So, if we believe that money is scarce, we create and experience scarcity in our lives. The dome of scarcity will move with you, and everything that represents abundance will stay out of your reach.

HEALTH

In this society, we've taken the term "health care" and completely turned it on its head. If you are a person who struggles with health, the first step would be to look at what you have been programmed to believe about health.

We are told to trust our doctors, ask our doctors what is right for us, and follow unquestioningly what our doctors tell us. We are told that we must get yearly health screenings, and in our current society, if you are someone who does not get these annual health screenings, you are treated like a crazy person.

Let's break down what health screenings really are: They aren't screening for health; they are screening for sickness or unhealth. Our entire medical industrial complex is far more concerned with keeping us sick than with maintaining our health. Health isn't profitable. The screenings are the gateway drug to becoming assimilated into the medical matrix.

It is our belief in unhealth that keeps us going back year after year to see if we're healthy. Do you see how this belief has our attention on unhealth? What do you think the dome will reflect back to you?

Health will remain a struggle for anyone who pours life energy into the idea that sickness and unhealth are the norm and that we need to take a pill, an injection, or undergo a screening to achieve health.

Health is natural. Health is what the body is amazing at if we get our minds out of the way.

This also applies to our current diet and exercise industries. We believe that we have to follow this diet or that exercise program to obtain optimum health.

In the same way, we are focusing our attention on the fact that we don't already have health and that there are all these things we need to strive and struggle to do to obtain it. If this is a core belief, you will continually struggle with health.

If you got rid of this belief that most people take for granted, you might find that your body responds in remarkable ways. You might discover that you begin exercising because you enjoy it or that your intuition naturally points to the types of foods you should eat for your unique body.

We are just making a point here about beliefs. We are not giving medical advice. (See, we have to say that because our society believes so strongly in its own delusion of sickness that we could get into serious legal trouble if we don't.)

About now, we would guess that the voice inside your head is disagreeing mightily with what you've just read. "That's utter nonsense and dangerous! People need their medicine!"

Notice the things that create the strongest reaction within you. That's a good place to start looking for where you put your energy.

REWARD AND PUNISHMENT

The character dome always reinforces the reward/punishment paradigm. This way of thinking is ingrained in our experience from birth. We are rewarded for "good" and punished for "bad."

We believe this so profoundly that we continue to reward or punish ourselves because we believe that's the way life works.

We also believe that we are separate entities from everything around us, and so we create the "out there" that rewards and punishes us as well.

In each of our examples above, the uniting theme is this reward and punishment belief.

The overproductive person believes that "punishment" will be the result if they stop doing so much. Punishment, in this case, would be losing the house, the car, the family, etc.

In our money example, the belief in this system shows up as well. Money is a reward for hard work, and lack of money is punishment for some perceived wrongdoing.

Our health example reflects this in the belief that health is something we have to do things to get; in other words, health is a reward and unhealth is a punishment.

In our view, this reward/punishment paradigm is one of the most difficult cycles to break. It keeps us trapped in our own little domes simply by our belief in it and the immense emotional energy we pour into it.

Are you beginning to see how limiting even our most 'normal' beliefs are? We limit our experience by putting energy into these systems rather than questioning and cutting the belief off from its power.

The world can only reflect back to you from the outside what you are putting energy into on the inside.

No belief is true. Overcome your fear of going within and questioning all the limitations that keep you from developing.

You CAN play this game differently. You CAN have a completely different experience, but the only way to get there is to go into the black hole inside and find out what's true.

MIND DOJO

MIND DOJO

Questions to Ponder

MONEY

Contemplate your financial situation. If it's good, write out why it's good and the beliefs that support your abundance.

If it's not so good, write out why it's not good. What beliefs are supporting your continued lack?

Take some time with this one. The issue of money is so interwoven into every area of our lives that unwinding this can take some time. You may find that it affects many areas of your life.

Some of the common limiting beliefs around money actually have their foundation in fear and unworthiness. They aren't really about money at all, except as the outward evidence of our internal beliefs.

Don't be afraid to dig deep into this money issue. Get radically honest about what your dome is reflecting back to you. It can only show you what's inside.

Here are some questions to get you started:

- What does money mean to you?
- Do you feel like you need to save money? Do you feel like money is scarce?
- Do you feel appreciation when you pay your bills?
- How do you feel about being in debt?
- Do you feel worthy of abundance and prosperity?
- Do you fear not having enough money? Why or why not?
- Do you fear having too much money? Why or why not?
- Do you value yourself based on your annual income?
- If you won the lottery, how would that feel? Would you continue to go to your job because you love it?
- If money were not a concern, what would you love to do with your life?
- Why do you think you can't do it now?

Journaling about these things can open our eyes to those hidden limits and beliefs. When we get ideas out on paper, we can look at them with more clarity.

EMPLOYMENT

If you have a job, do some journaling around it.

- Do you love what you do?
- If you had millions of dollars, would you still do it?
- Do you get your sense of self-worth from your job?
- If you don't like your job, what is the mirror showing you?
- What don't you like? Chances are, it's something within you that you are at odds with.
- If you like your job but have an issue with a co-worker or boss, what's the mirror showing you about yourself?

- Do you define yourself by your work?
- Do you feel like you have to work hard to be a good employee?
- Do you work long hours? Why or why not?
- Is your job a rich, rewarding experience?
- Is your job a chore?
- Are you excited to get back to it after your weekend?
- What would make your job better?

Pay attention to your responses; life can only reflect back to you what you're projecting. This type of work is key to finding those hidden limitations within you.

GAME RECAP

Now that we've looked at the things that make up our 'reality' and the structures that determine our perceived experience, let's bring it all together and look at it more holistically and recap the key concepts.

What folks commonly call the 'universe', we're referring to here as the game and the playing field. It's the world that you experience: the trees, the oceans, the cities and towns, and the appearance of other people.

The Ego structure (within it the Ego Character *as* the avatar), acts as the interface necessary to create the appearance of the playing field. In other words, the Ego is what makes everything appear in your reality; it is what makes your reality possible. Without the avatar or Ego structure, there is no playing field and there is no game.

The Ego structure is the code that the "game programmer" used to create the entire appearance of the game itself. It's through this interface that everything is experienced. It functions like the most advanced self-learning artificial intelligence in a way.

A good example of this would be if you were in a stark room with white walls; there's no furniture in the room, but there is a set of virtual reality goggles. When you put on the VR goggles, the white walls transform into the appearance of the entire universe, full of vibrant colors, sounds, smells, and textures. The VR goggles have all the programming within them to create this magical world, but they only work when you put them on and look through them. They are useless lying on the floor because there is nothing that they can create without the input of you observing through them. They are the necessary interface for everything to spring into being.

At level 1, the first objective is to build out the avatar by collecting and filtering that data, which begins to create a character dome around the avatar. The character is created from thoughts and beliefs, which in turn become more of a filter for the data to flow through. The data comes in, gets filtered through the character, and then projects back out those thoughts and beliefs for the character to experience as reality. The more limiting the belief filters are, the smaller our dome is, and the more limited the appearance of reality is.

The appearance can only reflect back the character construct. Since the character is formed at level 1, if we don't realize that at any time we can recreate the character construct, then we'll play at the same level for the entire game. When we understand that we can dismantle the thought and belief constructs, our character dome, we can then reach other levels of this wonderful game that we never dreamed existed.

Our belief structures are the core of the character, and they are made out of wispy thought stuff held together with emotion.

In other words, we dictate our universal environment. Our environment can only reflect back to us what we believe to be true at our core. The only way to change the outer experience is to change the core concepts on the inside. The game is your faithful servant. It is always reflecting back to you what you think you are. This is why we get such horrible results with mainstream manifesting. If we don't get to the core structure, the game can't give us anything different.

The game doesn't see things as good experiences or bad experiences, only experiences. And so, if you say "I am a millionaire" fifty times a day and only focus on your 'positive' thoughts but have the core concept of being unworthy, the game can only reflect back the unworthiness.

This is why we stress the importance of the core. If you don't question the core beliefs you're operating from, the game will always reflect the same things back to you. It's all it is designed to do.

When we begin to do the work to question the core programming, our beliefs, opinions, and judgments, then the game can and will adjust itself to the 'new core'. When the character dome is deconstructed, it changes the filter through which the data flows. When the filter changes, the experience changes.

In our human development analogy, when the character dome is fueled up and small because we have yet to develop out of it, the game reflects the same experience over and over again because that's all it can do. We function unconsciously as if we are asleep and have no idea that we are dreaming.

When we develop into adulthood, our dome is much bigger, and as we develop, it expands more and more, so the experience and playing field expand as well. We can have creative flow and nearly effortless functioning. We aren't using all of our life force to fuel the dome of our false identity any longer, and so we have that energy to use for other purposes. It could be said that we are now awake *within* the dream.

When we completely get rid of the dome, we are in an altogether different game. We are then awake *from* the dream.

Waking up *within* the game or the dream would be the equivalent of natural human development into adulthood.

Staying asleep or the unaware avatar is a much more dramatic production. That's where the roller coasters are and the drama of life or death and good vs. evil.

It's where we get to be offended, respected, romanced, taken advantage of, take advantage, self-sacrifice, strive, accomplish, fail, win, lose, and all of it has incredible meaning. This is what we mean when we say there is nothing wrong with you. This is how the game was designed: for you to play your part.

From our view now, we can't imagine why anyone would want to continue playing the game from such a severely limited perspective of the character dome. But that's because we aren't there anymore. When we were there, we couldn't imagine how it could be different; we just had an internal hunch that there was more than our limited view was showing us. That's why we search; that's why we go to the spiritual mall. We all inherently know that something is missing. We just don't have many folks who know what it is, and so no one can point the way.

Ego is what makes the game possible; it is the underlying structure of everything we perceive, and it makes the dream feel real. The character structure built around the Ego interface is what gives the experience its dramatic elements. In the context of gameplay, the character really isn't your enemy; it's just running a program, and without new data, it keeps running the same program.

When we are not conscious of this aspect of our lives, the character believes itself to be in charge, and that's a job it is not designed to do. If we want to operate differently in the game, the character must be dismantled and put in its rightful place of taking instruction rather than being in charge.

The character does not exist in truth. It is a construct built of beliefs, opinions, judgments, and attachments. It is your belief that it does exist *as* your identity that keeps it intact.

The character is designed to focus on the illusion of 'out there,' all things that appear to be outside of you.

You are your experience; you are your universe because it is only reflecting you back to yourself.

When we go to the spiritual mall, this is really the simplicity that most are searching for, but it isn't really sold in the mall.

All that religion and spirituality deal in is appearances. They do not deal with the core structure.

Religion will give you a god outside of yourself, a moral code, and a pretty severe reward/punishment system.

Spirituality will give you dimensions, the universe, unity consciousness, compassion, all is love, or ascension. It still has a reward/punishment system built in, but it's far more subtle.

Life is very much like a dream. You can dream differently if you are willing to do one simple thing: change your mind. We stay so stuck in our little domes where we think we know things that changing our minds is often the hardest thing we can do. Many people would rather kill themselves than consider the possibility of changing their minds.

The game is our reality where we can do anything. We can ride every ride in the park to our heart's content. We can climb every mountain and swim every stream.

We can build cities and monuments and create art with a thought. We can create drama, tragedy, heartbreak, and comedy, and most importantly, we can create meaning. Why in the world would anyone want to wake up from the dream of the avatar?

We aren't sure anyone really does want to wake up. We think the vast majority of folks want to pretend that they are awake within the dream. That's where the spiritual mall comes in. It advertises itself as awakening, but the reality is more along the lines of further sedation. There is nothing wrong with that; it's what the game is for.

If you want endless searching and never finding, then religion and spirituality are your go-to superstores. For many, the act of searching supplies the meaning in life.

Constant searching for what can never be lost also fuels the dramatic element of the game. People find meaning in the searching itself. It makes the character think it's 'getting somewhere' or that there is a 'path' to somewhere else, and it thinks it's making progress. The character gets to stay intact and find a deep well of specialness and meaning in this pursuit.

Developing into an adult is a solitary pursuit. You must go within, to your own black hole. You must ferret out your bullshit beliefs; you have to take your trash out so you can build the appropriate chrysalis in which to mature.

It's not an easy thing for a caterpillar to grow wings, and it won't be easy for you to fully mature either. But with just a little bravery, focus and white-hot intent, you can smash your dome and come out the other side as a new order of being.

It's really up to you. There is nowhere else to go; there is only here and now. How you experience here and now is the only thing you have.

You can start today. You can begin the process of changing your life experience. It all starts with questioning your beliefs and finding out where they came from and then perhaps you can see the structure of the ego-character so the chains of identification as the character can loosen.

SACRED SELF-DECEPTION

When we say this is a foundational book or a primer, it's because all you've just discovered is still from the ego-character identification viewpoint; it is still based in false separation and very much self-deception.

While this book deals strictly with the appearances that arise from the illusion of the separate self, it does so by showing the underlying structure. This is what spirituality and religion do not show because if you understand the structure and begin to see the illusory nature of the separate self, you become a much more discerning consumer, and you'll start asking questions that they cannot answer.

We hope that you now realize that every one of your beliefs is self-deception. Not just religious or spiritual beliefs, but ALL beliefs. Beliefs about who you are, what you do, what life is, what meaning is, what's important, what's right, wrong, good, and bad. None of your beliefs are true. They have no basis in fact.

Everything we *believe* we are is a construct of the character we play in the game. When you see this structurally, the identification as the character can loosen; this loosening is necessary to move on to the next book, **Awakening: The Sacred Art of Self-Destruction.**

The purpose of this book is to guide you into questioning what you think you know. It is to give you a foundation for further inquiry.

It is important to take a look at our beliefs; we used spiritual and religious beliefs because they are the easiest to use as examples. If you want to begin development into adulthood, you'll have to question beliefs that are far more ingrained than those.

Our identification as character is self-deception. Our perception of an "I" in here and a world out there is self-deception. But as we've seen, these self-deceptions are what provide the dramatic content of what we call life. Ego-character identification is not wrong, or of a 'lower vibration,' or better or worse than anything else, though many folks claim that it is. The only thing that could make that claim is Ego itself.

The greatest self-deception of all is the belief that you are a separate, independent being—separate from everything around you, separate from other people, separate from your environment, and separate from whatever you call a higher power.

You are not separate from what you might call 'the Universe' or 'God.' There is only one thing: we're calling it Consciousness in this book because it's a familiar term. In truth, there is no 'you' in here and a world out there, though it's a very convincing illusion.

With this in mind, are you beginning to see how and why we are able to be so bold in our shakedown of spirituality and religion? When it's clearly seen that the construct of a separate "I" is only made of thoughts and beliefs tied together with emotions, then honest inquiry into just 'who' we are can begin.

If there is no solid, concrete 'you,' how could there be a solid, concrete 'other' from which you can receive reward or punishment? There is no 'other' to purify yourself for, raise your frequency for, or don your light warrior armor for. There is difficulty in understanding this if we don't first expose the structure.

It was important to expose the basics of the structure before we dive into the next book, **Awakening: The Sacred Art of Self-Destruction,** where we go further. Out of adulthood and self-construction and into the great mystery of what Awakening actually is and the destruction of the self you've only just learned how to build.

It's a very different kind of book than this one. The Ego will have nowhere to hide, and you'll get a first-hand view into the components of the structure that hold it up, how it self-repairs, and you'll learn that there is no 'you' that can do anything about it.

ACKNOWLEDGMENTS

First of all, our heartfelt thanks go out to our imagined readers. If not for you, we would not have had the wonderful experience of expressing our thoughts.

We would also like to thank our amazing Publishing Company, Katana Publishing. Their support, patience, and unwavering belief in our project was and is priceless.

A very special shout-out to Sunseeds.life for their support of this project as well. We couldn't have done it without you!

Shadow would like to give her heartfelt gratitude and appreciation to her amazing husband Lucas. Lucas is my heart. He acts as my true north when navigating this strange new world gets confusing.

Lucas would like to say to Shadow… "Right back at you!"

Katana Publishing LLC

www.katanapublishing.net

"No Paths. No Truths. Cuts."

www.ingramcontent.com/pod-product-compliance
Lightning Source LLC
Chambersburg PA
CBHW070639160426
43194CB00009B/1511